SOUPS, STEWS
& OVEN LOVIN'
BREADS

D1016283

Ottenheimer Publishers, Inc.

Publisher: Sally Peters
Publication Manager: Diane B. Anderson
Senior Editor: Elaine Christiansen
Senior Food Editor: Jackie Sheehan
Test Kitchen Coordinator: Pat Peterson
Circulation Specialist: Karen Goodsell
Production Coordinator: Michele Warren
Publication Secretary: Mary Thell
Food Editor: Lola Whalen
Food Stylist: Susan Brosious
Food Stylist's Assistant: Lola Whalen
Contributing Editor: Patricia Miller
Consulting Editor: William Monn
Home Economists: Pillsbury Publications
Nutrition Information: Pillsbury Technology
Design: Tad Ware & Company, Inc.
Photography: Studio 3

Cover Photo: Microwave Corn Bread p. 70,
Garbanzo Bean Stew p. 38

Copyright 1990, 1994 by The Pillsbury Company.

Printed in the U.S.A.

**Reprinted by Ottenheimer Publishers, Inc.,
with permission from Classic® Cookbooks,
© 1994 THE PILLSBURY COMPANY. All rights reserved.**

Contents

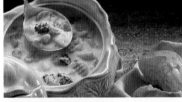

Special Features:

Flavorful 🫘 Bean Soups and Stews
Oven Lovin' 🌽 Cornmeal Recipes
🍲 Cook's Notes Throughout To
Increase Your Cooking Know-how!

Soups, Stews
and Oven Lovin'
Breads

Season to season or coast to coast, anytime, anyplace is best for savoring these good-for-you foods!

Soups and stews warm, sustain and soothe us. They whet our appetites, stick to our ribs and make us feel better when we're under the weather. They're simple or elegant, hearty or light. They're one-pot meals that need only breads fresh from the oven and crisp, green salads to be complete.

These nourishing foods have evolved through the centuries, from culture to culture. In this savory selection of recipes, there are those that reflect their ethnic origins, those that mirror a regional heritage of the United States, and those that are contemporary and inviting. Where possible, we've updated the cooking methods by incorporating food processor, blender and microwave directions. And we've included a glossary describing soups and stews plus a helpful handful of Cook's Notes and tips.

What better way to chase the chill from an end-of-winter day than with these foods that are so tempting, and so good for you, too!

One-pot preparation, the true beauty of soups and stews, needs only simple equipment as follows:

- A stockpot with tall, straight sides to allow the liquid to bubble up through the ingredients for optimum flavor. A tight-fitting cover, sturdy handles, and 12 to 24-quart capacity for large recipes are useful.

- A 5 to 6-quart Dutch oven or kettle with tight-fitting cover for stews or soups. A deep 10 to 12-inch covered frying pan or 3-quart saucepan can be used for small quantities. Keep in mind that pots should be heavy enough to prevent scorching.

- A large colander or cheesecloth for straining bones and vegetables from homemade broth.

- A knife that feels balanced and comfortable to you. A French chef's knife with an 8 to 10-inch blade will let you cut, chop, slice and dice with ease.

- A cutting board to protect counter top.

- A food processor, blender or food mill for chopping ingredients and pureeing soups.

- Utensils like a ladle, skimmer, whisk and large spoon.

Legumes: Flavorful and Full of Nutrition

John Steinbeck once wrote, "Beans are a roof over your stomach. Beans are a warm cloak against economic cold." That nutshell description just about covers the **benefits of dried beans and other legumes.** They are:

- Nutritious. High in complex carbohydrates, B vitamins, and dietary fiber; a good source of calcium, potassium, iron and magnesium; low in sodium and fat. When beans are combined with grains, pasta, meat, cheese or milk, all essential amino acids are present to provide complete protein.

- Economical. Legumes cost mere pennies per serving. A pound of dried beans measures about 2 cups which triples in volume when rehydrated and cooked.

- Delicious. More than 12 varieties, each with their own flavor and texture. Dried legumes include lentils and split peas, black-eyed peas, navy, Great Northern, lima, pinto, kidney beans and soybeans.

Despite differences in color and flavor, peas and beans of a similar type can be used interchangeably. However, dried legumes will never be considered a fast food.

All dried legumes, except for lentils and split peas, need to be soaked to rehydrate them before cooking.

Sort legumes before soaking. Sort them by rinsing in cold water and removing any damaged beans and foreign material.

There are two soaking methods: overnight or quick.

- Overnight: Place legumes in large container. For every pound (2 cups) of legumes, add 6 cups cold water. Let stand in a cool place for at least 6 hours or overnight. Drain and rinse.

- Quick: Place legumes in saucepan or Dutch oven large enough to allow expansion of beans. For every pound (2 cups) of legumes, add 6 to 8 cups cold water. Boil 3 minutes, cover and soak 1 to 4 hours, adding water as needed to keep beans covered. Drain and rinse, if desired.

To cook, place soaked, drained and rinsed beans in 3 to 4-quart saucepan. Add 6 cups of cold water, 2 tablespoons oil (to prevent foaming) and 2 teaspoons salt. Boil gently to avoid separation of skins until desired tenderness is reached, about 1 to 2 hours. For salads, beans should be more firm than those for soups or stews. For mashing or pureeing, cook until soft.

The soaking water can be used for cooking the beans. However, beans contain certain water soluble sugars that the body can't digest. In some people this causes flatulence (gas). To reduce the formation of gas, discard soaking water and cook beans in fresh water for half an hour. Discard that water, add fresh water and finish cooking. The disadvantage of discarding the soaking liquid is that it contains some nutrients.

Store dried legumes in an airtight container in a cool, dry place. **Store cooked beans** in the refrigerator for up to 2 to 3 days or freeze in containers. For best results, use dried legumes within a year of purchase. Older beans are drier and may never rehydrate completely.

Hard water and higher altitude may increase soaking and cooking times. Acidic ingredients such as vinegar, wine or tomatoes make beans firm and will lengthen the cooking time of beans. **Add acidic ingredients and salt when beans are almost cooked.**

Glossary of Terms
for Soups and Stews

Bisque   A rich cream or pureed soup, often made with shellfish, poultry or game.

Borscht   A soup made primarily of beets and served hot or cold with sour cream.

Bouillon   A seasoned broth in concentrated form.

Broth   The liquid obtained by simmering meat or poultry, bones and/or vegetables in water. Broth is usually seasoned, strained and degreased for use as the base for soups, stews and sauces. The terms broth and stock are used interchangeably.

Brunswick   A stew typically featuring two meats such as chicken and game plus vegetables.

Burgoo   A stew generally made from several kinds of meat, a variety of vegetables and highly spiced.

Cassoulet   A French-inspired meaty bean stew usually containing sausage and poultry. It is typically flavored with garlic.

Chili Con Carne   A highly seasoned Mexican-American dish of beef, tomatoes and sometimes beans. There are many variations, and the name is often shortened to chili.

Chowder   A milk-based thick soup made from fish, shellfish or vegetables. Diced potatoes are usually included.

Cioppino   A tomato-based fisherman's stew containing various kinds of seafood.

Consomme   A clear soup made by straining, reducing and clarifying broth.

Fricassee   A dish of cut-up pieces of meat (as chicken or veal) stewed in stock and served in a white sauce.

Gumbo   A thick Creole soup containing a combination of poultry, game, fish, seafood and vegetables. It is thickened with okra pods or gumbo filé, powdered dried sassafras leaves.

Minestrone A rich thick vegetable soup usually with dried beans and pasta.

Ragout   A well-seasoned meat and vegetable stew in a thick sauce.

Stew   A combination of meat or fish, vegetables, and a small amount of liquid that is simmered or slowly boiled in a covered container. It is characterized by tender meat and well-mingled flavors.

Stock   See Broth.

Soup's On

Soup's On

From first course to main course, satisfy with soup.

The types and tastes are legion, limited only by available ingredients and a sprinkling of the cook's imagination. Most soups have three things in common:

1. They're simple.

2. They're satisfying.

3. They begin with a broth.

Canned broth or bouillon cubes can be purchased, but broths that are simmered on the back of the range contribute character and body to homemade soups. These made-at-home broths also let *you* control the salt and fat content. Look for beef, chicken and vegetable broth recipes in this section, as well as a flavorful fish broth for fish soups and chowders.

Chilled Cucumber Soup is a refreshing first-course soup. Parsley and mint blend with the light flavors of this yogurt-based soup. Another meal-starter is *Pear-Brie Soup.* Serve this mellow, cream soup warm on a wintery evening as a complement to pork or poultry.

Soup can make a cozy meal for family or guests. *Heartland Beef and Vegetable Soup, Multi-Bean Soup,* and *Smoked Ham and Lentil Soup* are hearty and filling. They need only a green salad, sliced winter fruits and crusty bread to round out a perfect meal. Dress up a meal with compatible companion soups like *Cheddar Cheese Soup* and *Red Pepper Soup.* Pour a ladle of each simultaneously into a bowl from opposite sides. Swirl through the soups with a table knife for a decorative touch if you wish and voilá, easy elegance!

Pictured on previous page: Cheddar Cheese Soup and Red Pepper Soup

Serve this quick and easy cheese soup for a family meal or pour it into a thermos for a lunch away from home. As an elegant entertaining idea, this versatile soup can also be served as a companion to Red Pepper Soup.

Cheddar Cheese Soup

½ cup finely chopped onion
¼ cup finely chopped carrot
¼ cup finely chopped celery
3 cups vegetable broth or chicken broth
1 tablespoon cornstarch
2 tablespoons water
4 oz. (1 cup) diced sharp Cheddar cheese
10¾-oz. can condensed cream of potato soup
8-oz. jar pasteurized process cheese spread

In large saucepan, combine onion, carrot, celery and vegetable broth. Bring to a boil. Reduce heat; cover and simmer 10 minutes or until vegetables are tender.* In small bowl, combine cornstarch and water; mix well. Stir into broth mixture. Bring to a boil; reduce heat. Add Cheddar cheese, potato soup and cheese spread; whisk until cheese is melted and mixture is well combined. Heat gently; DO NOT BOIL. 6 (1-cup) servings.

TIP: *At this point, broth mixture can be pureed in blender or food processor until smooth.

NUTRITION INFORMATION PER SERVING

SERVING SIZE: 1 CUP		PERCENT U.S. RDA PER SERVING	
CALORIES	230	PROTEIN	20%
PROTEIN	12g	VITAMIN A	40%
CARBOHYDRATE	11g	VITAMIN C	2%
FAT	15g	THIAMINE	2%
CHOLESTEROL	45mg	RIBOFLAVIN	15%
SODIUM	1080mg	NIACIN	*
POTASSIUM	220mg	CALCIUM	35%
		IRON	2%

*Contains less than 2% of the U.S. RDA of this nutrient.

A sweet red pepper is a fully matured green bell pepper. Its distinctive flavor enhances this tomato-based soup.

Red Pepper Soup

3 large red bell peppers, halved lengthwise, seeded
2 tablespoons margarine or butter
1 medium onion, finely chopped
28-oz. can (3 cups) Italian plum tomatoes
1 cup dry red wine or beef broth
½ teaspoon dill weed
½ teaspoon salt
¼ teaspoon pepper
1 cup cocktail vegetable juice
¼ cup sliced green onions

Lay pepper halves, cut side down, on broiler pan. Broil 3 to 4 inches from heat about 15 minutes or until skin is completely blackened. Remove from pan. Place in plastic bag; let stand 10 minutes to steam. Peel pepper; finely chop.

Melt margarine in large saucepan over medium heat. Add onion; cook until tender. In blender container, puree tomatoes and chopped peppers. Add to onion. Blend in wine, dill weed, salt and pepper. Bring to a boil; reduce heat. Simmer 20 minutes, stirring occasionally. Stir in vegetable juice; simmer 5 minutes. Garnish with sliced green onions. 6 (1-cup) servings.

NUTRITION INFORMATION PER SERVING

SERVING SIZE: 1 CUP		PERCENT U.S. RDA PER SERVING	
CALORIES	120	PROTEIN	4%
PROTEIN	3g	VITAMIN A	110%
CARBOHYDRATE	14g	VITAMIN C	161%
FAT	4g	THIAMINE	10%
CHOLESTEROL	0mg	RIBOFLAVIN	8%
SODIUM	390mg	NIACIN	8%
POTASSIUM	610mg	CALCIUM	2%
		IRON	10%

Minestrone is a hearty Italian vegetable soup in a meat broth. We love to serve this short-order version with Herbed Oatmeal Pan Bread (see Index).

Pasta-Meatball Minestrone

- ½ lb. lean ground beef
- ½ lb. sweet Italian sausage
- 2 tablespoons Italian-seasoned dry bread crumbs
- 1 tablespoon grated Parmesan cheese
- ¼ teaspoon salt
- ¼ teaspoon pepper
- 1 egg
- ¼ cup chopped onion
- 1 garlic clove, minced
- ½ cup thinly sliced carrots
- 1 teaspoon Italian seasoning
- 3 cups beef broth or 3 cups hot water and 1 tablespoon beef-flavor instant bouillon
- 16-oz. can (2 cups) tomatoes, undrained, cut up
- ½ cup uncooked rotini (spiral macaroni)
- 1 small zucchini, sliced Grated Parmesan cheese

MICROWAVE DIRECTIONS: In large bowl, combine ground beef, Italian sausage, bread crumbs, 1 tablespoon Parmesan cheese, salt, pepper and egg; mix well. Form into ¾-inch meatballs; place in 3-quart microwave-safe casserole. Add onion and garlic. Cover and microwave on HIGH for 5 to 6 minutes or until meat is no longer pink, rearranging once halfway through cooking. Drain. Add remaining ingredients except zucchini and Parmesan cheese. Cover and microwave on HIGH for 10 minutes, stirring once halfway through cooking. Add zucchini; microwave on HIGH for 5 to 10 minutes or until vegetables and pasta are tender, stirring once halfway through cooking. Garnish as desired. Serve with Parmesan cheese. 5 (1½-cup) servings.

CONVENTIONAL DIRECTIONS: Combine and form meatballs as directed above. Heat **1 tablespoon oil** in 4 to 6-quart Dutch oven over medium heat. Cook meatballs, onion and garlic until meatballs are browned, turning frequently. Drain. Add remaining ingredients except zucchini and Parmesan cheese. Bring to a boil. Reduce heat; cover and simmer 10 minutes. Add zucchini; cook covered 5 minutes or until zucchini is crisp-tender and pasta is of desired doneness. Garnish as desired. Serve with Parmesan cheese.

NUTRITION INFORMATION PER SERVING

SERVING SIZE: 1-1/2 CUPS		PERCENT U.S. RDA PER SERVING	
CALORIES	260	PROTEIN	25%
PROTEIN	17g	VITAMIN A	80%
CARBOHYDRATE	16g	VITAMIN C	20%
FAT	14g	THIAMINE	20%
CHOLESTEROL	100mg	RIBOFLAVIN	10%
SODIUM	975mg	NIACIN	20%
POTASSIUM	550mg	CALCIUM	8%
		IRON	15%

Cook's Note
Skimming Fat from Broths and Soups

During cooking, the fat in meat and poultry liquefies and rises to the surface of broths and soups. To skim this fat from hot broths and soups, use a skimmer, spoon or baster. If the broth or soup can be chilled, the fat will solidify and will be easy to lift off.

Pasta-Meatball Minestrone

Fulfill that special craving for pizza on a cold winter's day with this quick and easy soup.

Family Pizza Soup

6 (½-inch) slices French bread
1 lb. ground beef
1 medium onion, sliced
1 garlic clove, finely chopped
¼ teaspoon fennel seed
¼ teaspoon oregano or ½ teaspoon oregano leaves
1 cup water
28-oz. can (3 cups) Italian plum or whole tomatoes, cut up, undrained
14-oz. jar pizza sauce
4-oz. can Green Giant® Mushrooms Pieces and Stems, if desired
3 oz. (3 slices) low-moisture part-skim mozzarella cheese, halved

Heat oven to 325°F. Trim slices of French bread to fit inside 2-cup ovenproof soup bowls. Place bread on ungreased cookie sheet. Bake at 325°F. for 20 to 25 minutes or until toasted. Remove from oven; increase oven temperature to 425°F.

Meanwhile, in large saucepan or Dutch oven brown ground beef with onion and garlic over medium heat; drain. Add all remaining soup ingredients except cheese. Bring to a boil. Reduce heat; simmer 10 minutes. Pour soup into oven-proof soup bowls; top each with slice of toasted French bread. Place 1 cheese slice on each toast slice. Place bowls on 15x10x1-inch baking pan. Bake at 425°F. for 3 to 5 minutes or until cheese melts. Serve immediately.
6 (1⅓-cup) servings.

TIP: Soup can be served in regular soup bowls. After bread has been toasted on cookie sheet for 20 to 25 minutes, place cheese slices on toasted bread slices. Bake at 325°F. for an additional 2 to 3 minutes until cheese starts to melt. Top each bowl of soup with cheese-topped toast slice.

NUTRITION INFORMATION PER SERVING

SERVING SIZE: 1-1/3 CUPS		PERCENT U.S. RDA PER SERVING	
CALORIES	310	PROTEIN	30%
PROTEIN	20g	VITAMIN A	25%
CARBOHYDRATE	25g	VITAMIN C	35%
FAT	15g	THIAMINE	10%
CHOLESTEROL	50mg	RIBOFLAVIN	20%
SODIUM	860mg	NIACIN	30%
POTASSIUM	530mg	CALCIUM	15%
		IRON	20%

Designed for children, this quick and easy soup is perfect served in a mug along with Oats 'n Wheat Blueberry Muffins.

Easy A-B-C Soup

2 cups cubed cooked chicken or turkey
2 cups Green Giant® Frozen Mixed Vegetables (from 16-oz. pkg.)
½ cup chopped celery
¼ cup chopped onion
¼ teaspoon thyme leaves
1 bay leaf
6 cups chicken broth
1 cup alphabet macaroni
Salt and pepper

In 4-quart saucepan or Dutch oven, combine chicken, mixed vegetables, celery, onion, thyme, bay leaf and broth. Bring to a boil; reduce heat and stir in macaroni. Simmer 12 to 15 minutes or until vegetables and macaroni are tender. Remove bay leaf; season to taste.
10 (1¼-cup) servings.

NUTRITION INFORMATION PER SERVING

SERVING SIZE: 1-1/4 CUPS		PERCENT U.S. RDA PER SERVING	
CALORIES	120	PROTEIN	15%
PROTEIN	11g	VITAMIN A	30%
CARBOHYDRATE	14g	VITAMIN C	2%
FAT	2g	THIAMINE	10%
CHOLESTEROL	25mg	RIBOFLAVIN	6%
SODIUM	445mg	NIACIN	20%
POTASSIUM	170mg	CALCIUM	2%
		IRON	6%

Colorful and light-bodied, this Italian soup has a pleasing pizza flavor. Make a sandwich while it simmers for a satisfying meal in about 30 minutes.

Pepperoni Tortellini Soup

1	cup uncooked cheese tortellini
1	garlic clove, minced
2 (14½-oz.)	cans low-salt chicken broth or chicken broth
14.5-oz.	can (1½ cups) no salt whole tomatoes or whole tomatoes, undrained, cut up
1	oz. (¼ cup) pepperoni slices, halved
8	fresh basil leaves, cut into strips, or 1 teaspoon basil leaves
2	tablespoons grated Parmesan cheese

In large saucepan, combine tortellini, garlic and chicken broth. Bring to a boil. Reduce heat; simmer until tortellini is of desired doneness, about 15 minutes. Stir in remaining ingredients except Parmesan cheese. Simmer an additional 5 minutes. Ladle soup into serving bowls; top each with Parmesan cheese. 4 (1¼-cup) servings.

NUTRITION INFORMATION PER SERVING

SERVING SIZE: 1-1/4 CUPS		PERCENT U.S. RDA PER SERVING	
CALORIES	170	PROTEIN	15%
PROTEIN	11g	VITAMIN A	30%
CARBOHYDRATE	15g	VITAMIN C	25%
FAT	7g	THIAMINE	10%
CHOLESTEROL	40mg	RIBOFLAVIN	10%
SODIUM	960mg	NIACIN	20%
POTASSIUM	350mg	CALCIUM	10%
		IRON	10%

Enjoy this hearty soup with Spoon Bread with Corn (see Index).

Hearty Bean and Pasta Soup

3½	cups water
½	cup elbow spaghetti or small ditalini pasta
½	cup chopped celery
9-oz.	cup Green Giant® Harvest Fresh® Frozen Baby Lima Beans or 8-oz. can butter beans, undrained*
1.15-oz.	envelope beefy onion dry soup mix
½	teaspoon basil leaves
16-oz.	can (2 cups) pork and beans, undrained
16-oz.	can (2 cups) whole tomatoes, undrained, cut up

Bring water to a boil in large saucepan or Dutch oven. Stir in pasta, celery, lima beans, soup mix and basil. Return to a boil. Reduce heat; simmer 7 to 10 minutes or until pasta is of desired doneness. Stir in pork and beans and tomatoes; cook until thoroughly heated. Garnish with shredded cheese, if desired. 5 (1½-cup) servings.

TIP: *If substituting 8-oz. can butter beans for frozen lima beans, add with pork and beans.

NUTRITION INFORMATION PER SERVING

SERVING SIZE: 1-1/2 CUPS		PERCENT U.S. RDA PER SERVING	
CALORIES	220	PROTEIN	15%
PROTEIN	11g	VITAMIN A	15%
CARBOHYDRATE	42g	VITAMIN C	20%
FAT	2g	THIAMINE	15%
CHOLESTEROL	5mg	RIBOFLAVIN	8%
SODIUM	1230mg	NIACIN	10%
POTASSIUM	790mg	CALCIUM	10%
		IRON	20%

Bacon adds flavor and appeal to this easy tomato soup. The soup can be garnished with basil cream in a star design for an attractive luncheon or first-course soup.

Country Tomato Soup with Basil Cream

28-oz.	can (3 cups) whole tomatoes, drained, reserving liquid
4	slices bacon, diced
½	cup finely chopped onion
½	cup (1 medium) finely chopped carrot
3	tablespoons flour or 4 teaspoons cornstarch
¼	teaspoon paprika
⅛	teaspoon white pepper
1¾	cups vegetable broth or 14½-oz. can less salt chicken broth

BASIL CREAM

2	tablespoons finely chopped fresh basil or 1 teaspoon basil leaves
⅓	cup dairy sour cream

Finely chop tomatoes; set aside. In large saucepan, cook bacon until crisp. Remove; set aside. Drain bacon drippings, reserving 1 tablespoon. Cook onion and carrot in reserved bacon drippings until tender. Stir in flour, paprika and white pepper. Cook 1 minute, stirring constantly. Gradually stir in vegetable broth and reserved tomato liquid. Bring to a boil. Reduce heat; add bacon and tomatoes. Simmer 10 minutes.

In small bowl, combine basil and sour cream. Ladle soup into warmed serving bowls. Gently spoon 1 heaping tablespoon basil cream into middle of each bowl.*
5 (1-cup) servings.

Pictured top to bottom: Jumbo Dilled Cornmeal Muffins p. 89, Country Tomato Soup with Basil Cream

TIP: *To make star pattern, allow basil cream to soften 1 minute after spooning on soup. With tip of knife, make a star pattern by pushing basil cream out from center to create points of star.

NUTRITION INFORMATION PER SERVING

SERVING SIZE: 1 CUP		PERCENT U.S. RDA PER SERVING	
CALORIES	130	PROTEIN	6%
PROTEIN	4g	VITAMIN A	90%
CARBOHYDRATE	14g	VITAMIN C	35%
FAT	6g	THIAMINE	10%
CHOLESTEROL	10mg	RIBOFLAVIN	6%
SODIUM	380mg	NIACIN	10%
POTASSIUM	480mg	CALCIUM	6%
		IRON	8%

Children will enjoy the American cheese flavor of this creamy, quick-to-prepare soup.

Potato Broccoli Soup

1	pkg. Pillsbury Creamy White Sauce Scalloped Potatoes
3	cups water
1	cup milk
2 (10¾-oz.)	cans condensed chicken broth
9-oz.	pkg. Green Giant® Harvest Fresh® Frozen Cut Broccoli, thawed
1	cup shredded American cheese or ½ cup crumbled blue cheese

In 5-quart Dutch oven, combine potato slices, contents of sauce mix envelope, water, milk and chicken broth; mix well. Bring mixture to a full boil. Reduce heat; cover and simmer 15 minutes, stirring occasionally. Cut large pieces of broccoli, if necessary. Add broccoli to potato mixture; simmer 5 to 7 minutes or until broccoli is crisp-tender. Gently stir in cheese until melted and well combined.
6 (1⅓-cup) servings.

NUTRITION INFORMATION PER SERVING

SERVING SIZE: 1-1/3 CUPS		PERCENT U.S. RDA PER SERVING	
CALORIES	220	PROTEIN	20%
PROTEIN	14g	VITAMIN A	10%
CARBOHYDRATE	23g	VITAMIN C	25%
FAT	8g	THIAMINE	4%
CHOLESTEROL	20mg	RIBOFLAVIN	15%
SODIUM	1380mg	NIACIN	20%
POTASSIUM	530mg	CALCIUM	25%
		IRON	6%

Hot and nourishing, this hearty soup has a tip for making your own bean mix. Select a variety of beans that suits your taste.

NUTRITION INFORMATION PER SERVING

SERVING SIZE: 1-1/2 CUPS		PERCENT U.S. RDA PER SERVING	
CALORIES	290	PROTEIN	25%
PROTEIN	17g	VITAMIN A	80%
CARBOHYDRATE	30g	VITAMIN C	20%
FAT	12g	THIAMINE	35%
CHOLESTEROL	25mg	RIBOFLAVIN	10%
SODIUM	940mg	NIACIN	15%
POTASSIUM	860mg	CALCIUM	8%
		IRON	20%

🫘 Multi-Bean Soup

2 cups dried bean mix*
Water
2 cups (¾ lb.) sliced smoked sausage
1 cup thinly sliced carrots
1 medium onion, chopped (about ¾ cup)
8 cups vegetable or beef broth
1 cup shredded savoy or green cabbage
1 teaspoon basil leaves
1 teaspoon oregano leaves
28-oz. can (3 cups) tomatoes, undrained, cut up
Salt

Sort beans. Rinse well; drain. Place in 6-quart stockpot; cover with water 2 inches above beans. Bring to a boil; boil for 2 minutes. Remove from heat; cover and let stand 1 hour.** Drain beans; add sausage, carrots, onion and broth. Bring to a boil. Reduce heat; cover and simmer until beans are tender but not mushy, about 30 minutes. Add cabbage, basil, oregano and tomatoes. Bring to a boil. Reduce heat; cover and simmer 20 minutes. Season to taste with salt. 10 (1½-cup) servings.

TIPS: *A variety of dried bean mixes are available in the produce, dried bean or bulk food sections of most supermarkets. You can prepare your own bean mix by blending a variety of beans such as navy beans, black-eyed peas, cranberry beans, garbanzo beans (chick peas), kidney beans, lima beans and pinto beans.

**An alternative method for hydrating the beans is soaking them in water overnight.

For a vegetarian soup, omit the sausage; add 4 oz. pasta or broken spaghetti before serving. Cook 8 to 10 minutes or to desired doneness.

This hearty soup has real family appeal and is guaranteed to chase away winter chills.

Heartland Beef and Vegetable Soup

1½ lb. ground beef
1 medium onion, sliced
½ cup uncooked regular rice*
1 teaspoon salt
1 teaspoon marjoram leaves
½ teaspoon garlic powder
6 cups beef broth
1 teaspoon Worchestershire sauce
16-oz. can (2 cups) stewed tomatoes, undrained
16-oz. pkg. Green Giant® American Mixtures® Heartland Style Frozen Broccoli, Cauliflower, and Carrots

In 5-quart Dutch oven, brown ground beef with onion over medium-high heat, breaking ground beef into ¾-inch pieces; stir occasionally. Drain well. Add all remaining soup ingredients except frozen vegetables. Bring to a boil. Reduce heat; cover and simmer 10 minutes, stirring occasionally. Add frozen vegetables; cook covered 10 minutes or until vegetables are crisp-tender. 8 (1¼-cup) servings.

Heartland Beef and Vegetable Soup with Croutons: Prepare soup as directed above. Heat oven to 250°F. To prepare croutons, spread one cut side of each bread slice with margarine. Sprinkle with garlic powder. Cut each slice into 25 cubes. Place on ungreased cookie sheet. Bake at 250°F. for 20 minutes or until crisp and lightly browned. Pour soup into serving bowls; top with croutons.

TIP: *Uncooked brown rice can be substituted for regular rice in this soup. Increase first simmer time to 25 minutes.

NUTRITION INFORMATION PER SERVING

SERVING SIZE: 1-1/4 CUPS WITH CROUTONS		PERCENT U.S. RDA PER SERVING	
CALORIES	280	PROTEIN	25%
PROTEIN	17g	VITAMIN A	35%
CARBOHYDRATE	21g	VITAMIN C	35%
FAT	14g	THIAMINE	10%
CHOLESTEROL	50mg	RIBOFLAVIN	10%
SODIUM	1050mg	NIACIN	25%
POTASSIUM	460mg	CALCIUM	6%
		IRON	15%

Use the pale, crisp stalks and the dark green, crimped leaves of the Chinese vegetable, bok choy, for this popular soup.

Oriental Vegetable Soup

6 cups chicken broth
6 slices fresh gingerroot
2 green onions, including tops, cut into 2-inch pieces
1 cup diagonally-sliced bok choy
1 cup fresh snow peas, diagonally sliced
½ cup sliced, drained bamboo shoots
½ cup sliced, drained water chestnuts
4.5-oz. jar Green Giant® Sliced Mushrooms, drained
1 tablespoon soy sauce
½ teaspoon sesame oil, if desired

In large saucepan, combine chicken broth, gingerroot and green onions. Bring to a boil. Reduce heat; cover and simmer 20 minutes. Remove and discard gingerroot and onion.* Stir in bok choy, snow peas, bamboo shoots, water chestnuts, mushrooms and soy sauce. Bring to a boil. Reduce heat; simmer 4 to 6 minutes or until vegetables are crisp-tender. Stir in sesame oil. 7 (1-cup) servings.

TIPS: *At this point, strips of uncooked chicken or turkey can be added to soup. Cook until tender. Continue as directed above.

Remaining bamboo shoots and water chestnuts from cans can be used in a salad or frozen with liquid in a covered container for future use.

NUTRITION INFORMATION PER SERVING

SERVING SIZE: 1 CUP		PERCENT U.S. RDA PER SERVING	
CALORIES	35	PROTEIN	2%
PROTEIN	2g	VITAMIN A	6%
CARBOHYDRATE	5g	VITAMIN C	21%
FAT	1g	THIAMINE	2%
CHOLESTEROL	0mg	RIBOFLAVIN	4%
SODIUM	520mg	NIACIN	2%
POTASSIUM	150mg	CALCIUM	2%
		IRON	4%

Around the world, chicken soup is touted for its healing properties.

Oriental Chicken Noodle Soup

1 cup chopped cooked chicken
⅛ to ¼ teaspoon ginger
⅛ teaspoon white pepper
2 oz. uncooked Chinese noodles
3 cups chicken broth
¼ cup chopped green onions, including tops
1 tablespoon rice wine vinegar or rice vinegar

In medium saucepan, combine chicken, ginger, white pepper, noodles and broth. Bring to a boil. Reduce heat; simmer 3 minutes, stirring to separate noodles. Remove from heat. Stir in green onions and vinegar. 2 (1¾-cup) servings.

NUTRITION INFORMATION PER SERVING

SERVING SIZE: 1-3/4 CUPS		PERCENT U.S. RDA PER SERVING	
CALORIES	270	PROTEIN	35%
PROTEIN	24g	VITAMIN A	15%
CARBOHYDRATE	20g	VITAMIN C	6%
FAT	10g	THIAMINE	10%
CHOLESTEROL	60mg	RIBOFLAVIN	10%
SODIUM	1150mg	NIACIN	40%
POTASSIUM	210mg	CALCIUM	2%
		IRON	10%

A flavorful smoked ham shank is preferred for this hearty soup. If using a ham bone, it may be necessary to add salt.

🫘 Smoked Ham and Lentil Soup

½ cup dry lentils
1¼-lb. smoked ham shank or ham bone
1 cup sliced carrots
1 cup chopped onions
¼ cup barley
1 large leek, chopped
1 teaspoon thyme leaves
3 medium strips lemon peel
2 bay leaves
8 cups water

Sort lentils. Rinse well; drain. In 5-quart Dutch oven, combine all soup ingredients. Bring to a boil. Reduce heat; cover and simmer for 1 hour or until lentils are tender but not mushy and meat pulls easily from bone. Remove and discard bay leaves and lemon peel. Remove ham shank; cool. Remove meat from bones; cut into bite-sized pieces. Add meat to soup. Cook until thoroughly heated, stirring occasionally. 6 (1½-cup) servings.

NUTRITION INFORMATION PER SERVING
SERVING SIZE: 1-1/2 CUPS

		PERCENT U.S. RDA PER SERVING	
CALORIES	150	PROTEIN	15%
PROTEIN	11g	VITAMIN A	120%
CARBOHYDRATE	22g	VITAMIN C	15%
FAT	2g	THIAMINE	20%
CHOLESTEROL	10mg	RIBOFLAVIN	6%
SODIUM	290mg	NIACIN	10%
POTASSIUM	380mg	CALCIUM	4%
		IRON	15%

Wild rice is a tasty partner for shrimp in this rich and delicious soup.

Shrimp Wild Rice Soup

½ cup uncooked wild rice, rinsed*
14½-oz. can chicken broth
2 (10¾-oz.) cans condensed cream of potato soup
2 cups half-and-half
1 cup shredded Swiss cheese
¼ cup sliced green onions
12-oz. pkg. frozen cooked shrimp
2 tablespoons sliced almonds, toasted**

In large saucepan, combine wild rice and chicken broth. Bring to a boil. Reduce heat; cover and simmer 40 to 50 minutes or until tender. Stir in potato soup. Add half-and-half, cheese and green onions. Simmer until cheese is melted, stirring frequently. Add shrimp; heat gently until shrimp are thoroughly heated, stirring occasionally; DO NOT BOIL. Garnish each serving with almonds. 6 (1⅓-cup) servings.

TIPS: *Uncooked regular rice can be substituted for part or all of the wild rice; reduce simmering time to 20 to 30 minutes or until rice is tender.

**To toast almonds, spread on cookie sheet; bake at 375°F. for 3 to 5 minutes or until light golden brown, stirring occasionally. Or, spread in thin layer in microwave-safe pie pan. Microwave on HIGH for 5 to 7 minutes or until light golden brown, stirring frequently.

NUTRITION INFORMATION PER SERVING
SERVING SIZE: 1-1/3 CUPS

		PERCENT U.S. RDA PER SERVING	
CALORIES	360	PROTEIN	40%
PROTEIN	25g	VITAMIN A	20%
CARBOHYDRATE	24g	VITAMIN C	2%
FAT	18g	THIAMINE	8%
CHOLESTEROL	160mg	RIBOFLAVIN	20%
SODIUM	1240mg	NIACIN	20%
POTASSIUM	450mg	CALCIUM	30%
		IRON	15%

Smoked Ham and Lentil Soup

Waxy red potatoes are recommended for use in chowders because they retain their shape.

Scallop and Vegetable Chowder

2 green onions, sliced
1 medium green bell pepper, diced
1 stalk celery, thinly sliced
1 tablespoon margarine or butter
½ teaspoon lemon pepper seasoning
½ teaspoon paprika
¼ teaspoon thyme or marjoram leaves
1 tomato, seeded, chopped
1 cup milk
1 medium cooked red potato, diced
¼ lb. (½ cup) small scallops
Salt

In medium saucepan, cook green onions, green pepper and celery in margarine until crisp-tender. Stir in seasoning, paprika, thyme and tomato. Cook over medium heat 3 minutes, stirring occasionally. Gradually stir in milk; cook until thoroughly heated. Add potato and scallops; simmer about 5 minutes or until scallops are opaque and tender. Season to taste with salt. 2 (1½-cup) servings.

📖 MICROWAVE DIRECTIONS: In 2-quart microwave-safe casserole, combine onions, green pepper, celery and margarine. Microwave on HIGH for 2 to 3 minutes or until crisp-tender, stirring once halfway through cooking. Stir in seasoning, paprika, thyme and tomato. Microwave on HIGH for 3 minutes or until very hot, stirring once halfway through cooking. Add milk. Microwave on HIGH for 1 minute. Stir in potato and scallops. Microwave on HIGH for 2½ to 4 minutes or until scallops are opaque and tender, stirring twice during cooking.

NUTRITION INFORMATION PER SERVING

SERVING SIZE:		PERCENT U.S. RDA	
1-1/2 CUPS		PER SERVING	
CALORIES	240	PROTEIN	25%
PROTEIN	16g	VITAMIN A	50%
CARBOHYDRATE	24g	VITAMIN C	90%
FAT	9g	THIAMINE	10%
CHOLESTEROL	30mg	RIBOFLAVIN	20%
SODIUM	470mg	NIACIN	10%
POTASSIUM	990mg	CALCIUM	20%
		IRON	10%

This pleasing full-bodied soup is great served warm or cold. Add warm rolls and a beverage for a delightful lunch.

Asparagus and Salmon Soup

10.5-oz. can Green Giant® Cut Spears Asparagus, undrained
Water
1 tablespoon margarine or butter
½ cup chopped onion
1 cup cubed, peeled potato
1 teaspoon chicken-flavor instant bouillon or 1 chicken-flavor bouillon cube
1 teaspoon chopped fresh dill weed or ½ teaspoon dill weed
¼ teaspoon white pepper
1 tablespoon lemon juice
2 cups half-and-half
7.5-oz. can pink or red salmon, drained, chunked

Drain asparagus, reserving liquid. Set asparagus aside. Add water to asparagus liquid to make 1 cup. Melt margarine in medium saucepan. Add onion; cook until tender, stirring occasionally. Stir in asparagus liquid, potato and bouillon. Bring to a boil. Reduce heat; cover and simmer 10 to 15 minutes or until potato is tender. In blender container or food processor bowl with metal blade, puree asparagus spears and potato mixture. Pour puree into 2-quart bowl; stir in dill weed, white pepper, lemon juice and half-and-half. Gently stir in salmon.* Cover;

refrigerate 2 to 3 hours or until thoroughly chilled. Stir before serving. Garnish with lemon twists or as desired. 4 (1¼-cup) servings.

TIP: *To serve soup warm, heat gently until thoroughly heated; DO NOT BOIL.

NUTRITION INFORMATION PER SERVING

SERVING SIZE: 1-1/4 CUPS		PERCENT U.S. RDA PER SERVING	
CALORIES	320	PROTEIN	25%
PROTEIN	15g	VITAMIN A	20%
CARBOHYDRATE	19g	VITAMIN C	25%
FAT	20g	THIAMINE	8%
CHOLESTEROL	60mg	RIBOFLAVIN	20%
SODIUM	660mg	NIACIN	20%
POTASSIUM	730mg	CALCIUM	25%
		IRON	8%

Refreshing cucumber soup is delightful as a first course. Garnish with a dollop of yogurt, twist of lemon and a mint sprig.

Chilled Cucumber Soup

½ cup loosely packed fresh parsley sprigs
¼ cup chopped green onions
2 tablespoons fresh mint leaves
2 large cucumbers, peeled, seeded, cut into chunks
1½ cups plain yogurt
1 cup chicken broth

🍲 FOOD PROCESSOR DIRECTIONS: In food processor bowl with metal blade, chop parsley, green onions and mint leaves. Add cucumber chunks; process until finely chopped. Add yogurt; process just to combine. Add chicken broth; process just to combine. Refrigerate soup at least 2 hours in covered container. Garnish as desired. 6 (1-cup) servings.

TIPS: Soup can be prepared in batches in blender.

To reduce calories and fat, substitute nonfat plain yogurt for plain yogurt.

NUTRITION INFORMATION PER SERVING

SERVING SIZE: 1 CUP		PERCENT U.S. RDA PER SERVING	
CALORIES	60	PROTEIN	6%
PROTEIN	4g	VITAMIN A	10%
CARBOHYDRATE	8g	VITAMIN C	20%
FAT	1g	THIAMINE	4%
CHOLESTEROL	4mg	RIBOFLAVIN	10%
SODIUM	115mg	NIACIN	2%
POTASSIUM	350mg	CALCIUM	15%
		IRON	6%

Mellow yet rich in flavor, this creamy fruit-flavored soup can be served in small portions to begin a meal.

Pear-Brie Soup

2 small pears (¾ lb.), peeled, halved, cored, chopped*
⅛ teaspoon ginger
⅛ teaspoon cinnamon
⅛ teaspoon cloves
2 cups chicken broth
2 tablespoons margarine or butter
2 tablespoons flour
5-oz. can (⅔ cup) evaporated milk
4 oz. Brie cheese, well chilled, rind removed, cut into small cubes
Nutmeg

In medium saucepan, combine pears, ginger, cinnamon, cloves and 1 cup of the chicken broth; mix well. Bring to a boil. Reduce heat; cover and simmer 15 to 20 minutes or until pears are tender. In food processor bowl with metal blade or blender container, puree mixture. Set aside.

Meanwhile, melt margarine in heavy saucepan over medium heat. Stir or whisk in flour. Add remaining chicken broth; cook and stir 1 minute. Gradually whisk in evaporated milk. Add cheese; whisk until melted and smooth. Stir in pear puree.** Heat gently; DO NOT BOIL. Sprinkle with nutmeg; garnish as desired. 8 (½-cup) servings.

TIPS: *A 16-oz. can pear slices, drained, can be substituted for fresh pears. Cook only until pears are thoroughly heated, about 5 minutes. Proceed as directed above.

**At this point, soup can be refrigerated in a covered container. Reheat just before serving.

NUTRITION INFORMATION PER SERVING

SERVING SIZE: 1/2 CUP		PERCENT U.S. RDA PER SERVING	
CALORIES	110	PROTEIN	8%
PROTEIN	5g	VITAMIN A	6%
CARBOHYDRATE	7g	VITAMIN C	*
FAT	7g	THIAMINE	2%
CHOLESTEROL	15mg	RIBOFLAVIN	8%
SODIUM	245mg	NIACIN	*
POTASSIUM	125mg	CALCIUM	8%
		IRON	*

*Contains less than 2% of the U.S. RDA of this nutrient.

A borscht is a soup of Russian origin made primarily of beets and is served hot or cold. This first-course version combines cranberry sauce and sour cream with the beets for tangy flavor and creamy pink color.

Cranberry Borscht

16-oz. can beets, undrained
16-oz. can jellied cranberry sauce
    1 cup water
    1 cup dairy sour cream
    1 tablespoon lemon juice
      Dairy sour cream, if desired

In food processor bowl with metal blade or blender container, process beets and cranberry sauce until pureed. (If using blender container, puree in batches.) Transfer to large saucepan; stir in water. Cook over medium heat until thoroughly heated and cranberry sauce is melted. Whisk in sour cream and lemon juice.* Top each serving with a dollop of sour cream; garnish as desired. 10 (½-cup) servings.

▥ MICROWAVE DIRECTIONS:
Puree beets and cranberry sauce as directed above. Transfer to 8-cup microwave-safe measuring cup or 2-quart casserole. Microwave uncovered on HIGH for 5 to 7 minutes or until mixture is thoroughly heated and cranberry sauce melts. Continue as directed above.

TIPS: *To serve soup cold, pour into container; cover. Refrigerate until chilled.

Four medium fresh beets (1½ to 2 lb.), peeled, grated and cooked in 2 cups water, can be substituted for canned beets. Process cooked beet mixture with cranberry sauce and continue as directed above.

NUTRITION INFORMATION PER SERVING

SERVING SIZE: 1/2 CUP		PERCENT U.S. RDA PER SERVING	
CALORIES	170	PROTEIN	2%
PROTEIN	2g	VITAMIN A	6%
CARBOHYDRATE	22g	VITAMIN C	4%
FAT	8g	THIAMINE	*
CHOLESTEROL	15mg	RIBOFLAVIN	4%
SODIUM	150mg	NIACIN	*
POTASSIUM	135mg	CALCIUM	4%
		IRON	2%

*Contains less than 2% of the U.S. RDA of this nutrient.

Pictured top to bottom: Cranberry Borscht, Pronto Pumpernickel p. 85

Use this broth as an economical substitute for chicken or beef broth in pureed or cream soups or as cooking liquid for meat soups or stews.

Vegetable Broth

- 2 large leeks (about 1½ lb.)
- 3 large celery stalks, including leaves, quartered
- 1 large Spanish or Bermuda onion, cut into chunks
- 3 large carrots, quartered
- 2 garlic cloves
- ½ lb. green beans, broken in half, if desired
- 12 cups cold water
- ½ cup firmly packed fresh parsley sprigs
- 3 sprigs fresh thyme or 1 teaspoon thyme leaves
- 1 bay leaf
- 8 peppercorns
  Salt

Cut root ends off leeks; remove and discard coarse outer leaves. Cut off and discard coarse ends of green tops. Split lengthwise, cutting to about 1 inch of root end. Separate and rinse leaves under running water; drain. Cut into 1-inch chunks.

In food processor bowl with metal blade, coarsely chop leeks and celery with on-off pulses. Transfer to stockpot or 5-quart Dutch oven. Coarsely chop onion, one half at a time, using on-off pulses. Add to stockpot. Process carrots and garlic cloves for 30 to 45 seconds or until chopped; add to stockpot along with green beans. Add water; bring to a boil. Reduce heat. Skim any foam from the surface. Add parsley, thyme, bay leaf and peppercorns. Cover; simmer gently 1 hour. Strain broth; discard vegetables. Season to taste with salt. Cool uncovered in refrigerator. Cover and store in refrigerator up to 4 days or freeze up to 6 months. 10 cups.

NUTRITION INFORMATION: Variables in this recipe make it impossible to calculate nutrition information.

This full-flavored broth can either be used as a soup base or served as is. It can be prepared months ahead and frozen for later use.

Beef Broth

- 2 lb. meaty beef bones, such as shank, cut into 3-inch pieces, or short ribs
- 2 lb. beef bones, such as knuckle, cracked
- 1 cup cut-up carrots
- 2 celery stalks with leaves, cut into 2-inch pieces
- 2 small onions, quartered
- 10 cups water
- 8-oz. can (1 cup) tomatoes, undrained, cut up
- 1½ teaspoons salt
- ½ teaspoon thyme leaves
- 5 peppercorns
- 2 fresh parsley sprigs
- 1 garlic clove, pressed
- 1 bay leaf
- ¾ teaspoon salt

Heat oven to 450°F. Place all bones in large roasting pan. Bake uncovered at 450°F. for 30 minutes. Add carrots, celery and onions. Bake, turning bones and vegetables occasionally, an additional 45 to 60 minutes or until bones are very deep brown (not charred).

Transfer ingredients from roasting pan to 8-quart stockpot or two 5-quart Dutch ovens. Discard fat in roasting pan. Add 2 cups of the water to roasting pan; heat and scrape to loosen any browned meat drippings. Pour hot liquid and remaining water over bones and vegetables in stockpot. Bring to a boil. Reduce heat; simmer partially covered 30 minutes. Skim off any residue that rises to the surface. Add remaining ingredients except ¾ teaspoon salt; simmer partially covered an additional 5 hours. Remove bones; strain broth. Stir in ¾ teaspoon salt. Cool uncovered in refrigerator. Cover and store in refrigerator up to 3 days or freeze up o 6 months. Skim fat from broth before using in recipe. 7 cups.

NUTRITION INFORMATION: Variables in this recipe make it impossible to calculate nutrition information.

Homemade chicken broth has a texture and richness that few commercial products can equal. The less expensive parts of the chicken are used. Older hens, labeled stewing hens, produce an especially rich and delicious broth. You will find that chicken broth is an ingredient in at least half the soups and stews in this book.

Chicken Broth

2 lb. chicken backs, necks and/or wings
8 cups water
2 small onions, quartered
1 cup coarsely chopped celery with leaves
½ cup sliced carrots
2 teaspoons chopped fresh parsley
1 teaspoon salt
¼ teaspoon pepper
1 bay leaf
½ teaspoon salt

In 5-quart Dutch oven, combine chicken and water. Bring to a boil. Skim off any residue that rises to the surface. Reduce heat; simmer partially covered 30 minutes. Add remaining ingredients except ½ teaspoon salt; simmer partially covered an additional 4 hours. Remove bones; strain broth. Stir in ½ teaspoon salt. Cool uncovered in refrigerator. Cover and store in refrigerator up to 3 days or freeze up to 6 months. Skim fat from broth before using in recipe. 8 cups.

NUTRITION INFORMATION: Variables in this recipe make it impossible to calculate nutrition information.

Make your own fish broth to add a subtle flavor to soup or chowders. Lean, mild-flavored white-fleshed fish like sole, flounder, halibut, whiting, pike or striped bass provide the best flavor.

Fish Broth

2 to 3 lb. fish bones and/or fish heads, rinsed, cut into 4-inch pieces
2 celery stalks, chopped
1 medium onion, sliced
1 carrot, sliced
1 lemon slice
7 to 8 cups water
¼ cup dry white wine, if desired
¼ cup firmly packed fresh parsley sprigs or 2 tablespoons parsley flakes
4 fresh thyme sprigs or 1 teaspoon thyme leaves
1 bay leaf
6 whole white peppercorns, if desired
Salt

In stockpot or 6-quart Dutch oven, combine fish bones, celery, onion, carrot and lemon. Add enough water to cover bones and vegetables. Stir in wine. Bring to a boil; reduce heat. Skim off any residue that rises to the surface. Add parsley, thyme, bay leaf and peppercorns. Simmer 30 minutes, skimming surface as necessary. Strain broth. Season with salt to taste. Cool uncovered in refrigerator. Cover and store in refrigerator up to 3 days or freeze up to 1 month. 6 cups.

TIP: Fish-flavor bouillon cubes can be substituted for fish broth by following package directions. Fish-flavor bouillon cubes are available in most large supermarkets.

NUTRITION INFORMATION: Variables in this recipe make it impossible to calculate nutrition information.

Satisfying Stews

Satisfying Stews

Make a marvelous meal in only one pot.

What's a stew to you? Is it a concoction of meat, vegetables, and potatoes cooked in a cast iron kettle until it's hearty and thick enough to stand a spoon upright? Or is it a kissing cousin to soup, an elegant, rich broth studded with seafood? Whatever your definition, you'll find the stew for you in this chapter.

If time is of the essence, *Quick Paella Stew,* based on the traditional Spanish dish of chicken, seafood and saffron, cooks in just 30 minutes. *Garbanzo Bean Stew* takes only minutes to prepare on top of the range or in the microwave. It's rich with nut-like garbanzo beans, spinach, tomatoes and oriental noodles.

When you've got time to spare, sit back and savor the scents of a simmering stew. *Beef Ragout,* seasoned with cinnamon and hearty red wine, is thick, rich and ready to eat in just over two hours. Or, combine the ingredients of *Six-Can Slow Cooker Chili* in minutes in a slow cooker, then forget about it and let the flavors meld for up to four hours. Oven stews, like *Rich Oven Veal Stew* and *Oven Chicken Stew,* are a snap to prepare and offer tasty, robust eating.

Pictured on previous page, left to right:
Fanfare Seafood Stew, Sesame and Basil
Rounds p. 75

Traditional stews are simmered slow. This stir-fried stew is fast to make and low in fat, cholesterol and calories. For a complete meal serve it with linguini or brown rice.

Fanfare Seafood Stew

8-oz. pkg. fresh or frozen haddock or cod fillets, thawed
¼ cup cream sherry or cooking sherry
1 tablespoon finely chopped gingerroot
½ teaspoon salt
⅛ teaspoon freshly ground black pepper
1 garlic clove, finely chopped
8 oz. large uncooked fresh or frozen shrimp, thawed, shelled and deveined
1 tablespoon olive or peanut oil
1½ cups fish broth or water
1 tablespoon soy sauce
16-oz. pkg. Green Giant® American Mixtures® San Francisco Style Frozen Broccoli, Carrots, Water Chestnuts and Red Peppers
4 teaspoons cornstarch
2 tablespoons cold water

Cut fillets into 1-inch cubes. In large bowl, combine cream sherry, gingerroot, salt, pepper and garlic; mix well. Add fish and shrimp; toss to coat. Let stand 20 minutes at room temperature. Drain; reserving marinade.

Heat oil in Dutch oven or wok over medium-high heat. Add fish and shrimp; stir-fry until opaque, 2 to 3 minutes. Remove; keep warm. Add fish broth, soy sauce and reserved marinade to Dutch oven; mix well. Add vegetables; bring to a boil. Reduce heat; cover and simmer 5 to 7 minutes or until vegetables are crisp-tender. In small bowl, combine cornstarch and water; mix well. Stir into stew. Cook until thickened, about 1 minute. Stir in fish and shrimp. Cook until thoroughly heated. 6 (1¼-cup) servings.

NUTRITION INFORMATION PER SERVING

SERVING SIZE: 1-1/4 CUPS		PERCENT U.S. RDA PER SERVING	
CALORIES	130	PROTEIN	20%
PROTEIN	15g	VITAMIN A	50%
CARBOHYDRATE	9g	VITAMIN C	50%
FAT	3g	THIAMINE	2%
CHOLESTEROL	65mg	RIBOFLAVIN	4%
SODIUM	480mg	NIACIN	10%
POTASSIUM	360mg	CALCIUM	4%
		IRON	8%

This tasty combination uses canned beans as very nutritious and economical extenders. Zesty Cheese Comb Bread (see Index) is all that's needed to complete this one-dish meal.

Sausage Bean Stew

2 lb. bulk pork sausage
4 cups water
2 (16-oz.) cans (4 cups) whole tomatoes, undrained, cut up
2 (15½-oz.) cans red kidney beans, undrained
15½-oz. can Great Northern beans, drained
2 medium onions, chopped
2 medium potatoes, peeled, cubed
½ cup chopped green bell pepper
½ teaspoon salt
½ teaspoon thyme leaves
¼ teaspoon garlic powder
1 large bay leaf

Brown sausage in Dutch oven, stirring to crumble; drain. Stir in remaining ingredients; bring to a boil. Reduce heat; cover and simmer 1 hour. Remove bay leaf. 9 (1½-cup) servings.

NUTRITION INFORMATION PER SERVING

SERVING SIZE: 1-1/2 CUPS		PERCENT U.S. RDA PER SERVING	
CALORIES	360	PROTEIN	30%
PROTEIN	19g	VITAMIN A	10%
CARBOHYDRATE	36g	VITAMIN C	40%
FAT	16g	THIAMINE	40%
CHOLESTEROL	40mg	RIBOFLAVIN	15%
SODIUM	1240mg	NIACIN	20%
POTASSIUM	1060mg	CALCIUM	10%
		IRON	20%

This famous French-style bean casserole typically requires numerous meats and a fairly long cooking procedure. The ingredients and process have been simplified here without compromising that great robust flavor.

Country French Cassoulet

- 1 lb. smoked sausage links, cut in half crosswise
- ¼ cup flour
- 1 teaspoon salt
- ½ teaspoon pepper
- 2½ lb. beef stew meat, cut into 1-inch cubes
- 3 medium onions, coarsely chopped (1½ cups)
- 3 garlic cloves, minced
- ¾ cup stuffed green olives, halved
- ½ to 1 teaspoon thyme leaves
- 2 (15½-oz.) cans kidney beans, drained
- 2 (4.5-oz.) jars Green Giant® Whole Mushrooms, undrained
- 2 to 3 cups dry red wine

Brown sausages in 5-quart Dutch oven. Remove from pan with slotted spoon; set aside. Meanwhile, in large bowl or plastic bag combine flour, salt and pepper. Add beef stew meat; toss or shake to coat. Add beef, onions and garlic to Dutch oven; cook until beef is evenly browned and onions are tender.

Heat oven to 350°F. In 5-quart deep earthenware casserole or ovenproof Dutch oven, combine sausages, beef mixture and remaining ingredients except wine. Add 2 cups wine. Cover; bake at 350°F. for 3 to 3½ hours or until meat is tender, stirring occasionally and adding more wine if necessary. Casserole

may be uncovered during last 45 minutes to thicken cassoulet, if desired. 9 (1-cup) servings.

NUTRITION INFORMATION PER SERVING

SERVING SIZE: 1 CUP		PERCENT U.S. RDA PER SERVING	
CALORIES	540	PROTEIN	70%
PROTEIN	46g	VITAMIN A	*
CARBOHYDRATE	23g	VITAMIN C	10%
FAT	23g	THIAMINE	40%
CHOLESTEROL	110mg	RIBOFLAVIN	30%
SODIUM	1410mg	NIACIN	45%
POTASSIUM	1010mg	CALCIUM	6%
		IRON	35%

*Contains less than 2% of the U.S. RDA of this nutrient.

Serve with a crisp green salad and crusty French bread for a complete meal.

Mostaccioli Beef Stew

- 1½ lb. beef stew meat, cut into 1-inch cubes
- 2 tablespoons oil
- 1 teaspoon salt
- 1 teaspoon paprika
- ½ teaspoon chili powder
- 2½ cups water
- 16-oz. can (2 cups) whole tomatoes, cut up, undrained
- 1 cup sliced carrots
- ½ cup sliced celery
- 1 medium onion, sliced
- 1 cup uncooked mostaccioli

In Dutch oven, brown meat in hot oil. Add remaining ingredients except mostaccioli; mix well. Cover and simmer for 2 hours or until meat is tender. Stir in mostaccioli; cook 12 to 15 minutes or until tender. 5 (1-cup) servings.

NUTRITION INFORMATION PER SERVING

SERVING SIZE: 1 CUP		PERCENT U.S. RDA PER SERVING	
CALORIES	330	PROTEIN	50%
PROTEIN	34g	VITAMIN A	160%
CARBOHYDRATE	21g	VITAMIN C	20%
FAT	12g	THIAMINE	20%
CHOLESTEROL	80mg	RIBOFLAVIN	20%
SODIUM	660mg	NIACIN	40%
POTASSIUM	830mg	CALCIUM	4%
		IRON	25%

A ragout is a highly seasoned stew of meat and vegetables in a thick sauce. Burgundy wine and cinnamon flavor this recipe.

Beef Ragout

¼ cup flour
2 teaspoons salt
¼ teaspoon pepper
2 lb. beef stew meat
2 medium onions, sliced
2 tablespoons oil
1 cup burgundy wine, dry red wine or water
½ cup water
1 beef-flavor bouillon cube or 1 teaspoon beef-flavor instant bouillon
1 bay leaf
1 cinnamon stick, if desired
4 medium carrots, sliced
2 stalks celery, chopped
4-oz. can Green Giant® Mushrooms Pieces and Stems, undrained

In 1 gallon plastic bag, combine flour, salt and pepper; add meat pieces. Shake to coat. In large skillet or Dutch oven, brown meat and onions in oil. Add burgundy wine, water, bouillon, bay leaf and cinnamon stick. Bring to a boil. Reduce heat; cover and simmer 1½ hours. (For milder cinnamon flavor, remove cinnamon stick after ½ to 1 hour.) Stir in carrots, celery and mushrooms. Cook for an additional 30 minutes or until meat and vegetables are tender. Remove cinnamon stick and bay leaf.
6 (1-cup) servings.

TIP: If desired, add 2 to 3 medium potatoes, peeled and cut into pieces, along with carrots.

NUTRITION INFORMATION PER SERVING

SERVING SIZE: 1 CUP		PERCENT U.S. RDA PER SERVING	
CALORIES	330	PROTEIN	60%
PROTEIN	36g	VITAMIN A	270%
CARBOHYDRATE	13g	VITAMIN C	10%
FAT	11g	THIAMINE	15%
CHOLESTEROL	90mg	RIBOFLAVIN	25%
SODIUM	1040mg	NIACIN	35%
POTASSIUM	800mg	CALCIUM	4%
		IRON	25%

Serve this stew in a deep platter and sprinkle it with fresh parsley, chervil or a combination of herbs. Any green vegetable would be a delicious accompaniment.

Rich Oven Veal Stew

½ cup Pillsbury's BEST® All Purpose or Unbleached Flour
½ teaspoon salt
½ teaspoon nutmeg
¼ teaspoon white pepper
2 lb. lean boneless veal, cubed
¼ cup margarine or butter
1 tablespoon oil
2 cups dry white wine or beef broth
8 small new red potatoes
3 carrots, cut into ½-inch slices
2 medium onions, quartered
½ lb. large fresh mushrooms, quartered
½ cup dairy sour cream
Salt

Heat oven to 350°F. Lightly spoon flour into measuring cup; level off. In 1 gallon plastic bag, combine flour, ½ teaspoon salt, nutmeg and white pepper; shake to mix. Add veal cubes; shake to coat. In 4-quart Dutch oven or heavy flameproof casserole, brown veal in margarine and oil. Stir in wine, potatoes, carrots, onions and mushrooms. Bring to a boil; remove from heat. Cover and bake at 350°F. for 1½ hours or until meat and vegetables are tender. Stir sour cream into stew. Season to taste with salt. 6 (1⅓-cup) servings.

NUTRITION INFORMATION PER SERVING

SERVING SIZE: 1-1/3 CUPS		PERCENT U.S. RDA PER SERVING	
CALORIES	540	PROTEIN	50%
PROTEIN	33g	VITAMIN A	210%
CARBOHYDRATE	28g	VITAMIN C	18%
FAT	26g	THIAMINE	20%
CHOLESTEROL	115mg	RIBOFLAVIN	30%
SODIUM	460mg	NIACIN	45%
POTASSIUM	950mg	CALCIUM	6%
		IRON	30%

This recipe features colorful abundant bell peppers in a scrumptious sweet-sour stew.

Three-Pepper Meatball Stew

1 lb. ground beef
¼ cup finely chopped onion
2 tablespoons oat bran
½ teaspoon salt
⅛ teaspoon pepper
2 teaspoons soy sauce
1 egg
2 tablespoons oil
⅓ cup uncooked regular long grain rice
2½ cups water
¼ cup sugar
¼ cup cider vinegar
1 medium green bell pepper, cut into 1½ by 1-inch pieces
½ red bell pepper, cut into 1½ by 1-inch pieces
½ yellow bell pepper, cut into 1½ by 1-inch pieces
5-oz. can pineapple juice
1 tablespoon cornstarch
2 tablespoons soy sauce

In large bowl, combine ground beef, onion, oat bran, salt, pepper, 2 teaspoons soy sauce and egg; blend well. For each meatball, use about 1 tablespoon mixture; shape into ball. In Dutch oven or large skillet, brown meatballs in oil; drain. Add rice and water. Bring to a boil. Reduce heat; cover and simmer until rice is tender, 13 to 14 minutes. Stir in sugar, vinegar, peppers and pineapple juice. Bring to a boil. Reduce heat; cover and simmer 5 minutes or until peppers are crisp-tender. In small bowl, combine cornstarch and 2 tablespoons soy sauce; mix well. Stir into meatball mixture. Cook over medium heat until mixture boils and thickens, stirring frequently.
4 (1¼-cup) servings.

Three-Pepper Meatball Stew

NUTRITION INFORMATION PER SERVING

SERVING SIZE: 1-1/4 CUPS		PERCENT U.S. RDA PER SERVING	
CALORIES	470	PROTEIN	35%
PROTEIN	23g	VITAMIN A	15%
CARBOHYDRATE	40g	VITAMIN C	70%
FAT	24g	THIAMINE	10%
CHOLESTEROL	140mg	RIBOFLAVIN	10%
SODIUM	1040mg	NIACIN	30%
POTASSIUM	460mg	CALCIUM	4%
		IRON	20%

Cook's Note

Storing Soups and Stews

• Refrigerate soups and stews immediately for quick and thorough cooling to avoid spoilage.

• For short-term storage of 3 days or less, refrigerate soups and stews in plastic or glass containers with airtight lids.

• For long-term storage, freeze in single-serving or family-sized freezer containers allowing 1½ inches of space at the top of each container. Label containers, freeze them promptly and plan to use the soup or stew within 4 months. Soups and stews made with beans, vegetables or meats retain flavor and texture well when frozen and reheated. It is best to add thickening during reheating for soups and stews thickened with flour or egg. Recipes featuring eggs, cheese and seafood are not recommended for freezing.

• To thaw frozen soups and stews, place container in refrigerator overnight or use microwave on defrost setting. Thawing soups before reheating is recommended.

• When reheating, slowly heat only the amount to be served. The microwave is useful for reheating.

Pork-Sweet Potato Stew

⅓ cup flour
2 tablespoons brown sugar
2 lb. boneless pork, cut into
   1-inch cubes
3 tablespoons Dijon mustard
3 tablespoons oil
2 garlic cloves, minced
1¾ cups chicken broth
¼ cup dry sherry or chicken
   broth
½ teaspoon salt
½ teaspoon pepper
4 small onions, peeled,
   quartered
2 medium sweet potatoes,
   peeled, cut into 1-inch
   cubes (3 cups)
½ cup loosely packed fresh
   parsley sprigs

In 1 gallon plastic bag, combine flour and brown sugar; shake to mix. In medium bowl, combine pork and mustard; mix well. Add to flour mixture in bag; shake to coat. Heat oil in 5-quart Dutch oven over medium heat. Add coated pork and garlic; cook until pork is evenly browned. Drain fat. Add broth and sherry. Bring to a boil. Boil 1 minute, scraping brown bits off bottom of Dutch oven. Reduce heat; cover and simmer 30 minutes. Add salt, pepper, onions and sweet potatoes; mix well. Cover and simmer 30 minutes or until vegetables are tender. Stir in parsley. 6 (1-cup) servings.

TIP: A 23-oz. can of yams, drained, can be substituted for fresh sweet potatoes. Add to stew 20 minutes after addition of onions.

NUTRITION INFORMATION PER SERVING

SERVING SIZE: 1 CUP		PERCENT U.S. RDA PER SERVING	
CALORIES	500	PROTEIN	50%
PROTEIN	35g	VITAMIN A	270%
CARBOHYDRATE	30g	VITAMIN C	30%
FAT	24g	THIAMINE	70%
CHOLESTEROL	110mg	RIBOFLAVIN	35%
SODIUM	610mg	NIACIN	40%
POTASSIUM	700mg	CALCIUM	4%
		IRON	15%

Traditional paella is a Spanish rice dish seasoned with saffron that includes chicken and a variety of seafood.

Quick Paella Stew

1 cup chopped celery
½ cup chopped onion
1 tablespoon chicken-flavor
   instant bouillon or
   3 chicken-flavor
   bouillon cubes
¼ teaspoon oregano leaves
¼ teaspoon saffron
2 garlic cloves, finely
   chopped
3 cups water
14½-oz. can (1½ cups) tomatoes,
   undrained, cut up
1 cup cubed cooked
   chicken
1 lb. fresh medium
   uncooked shrimp,
   peeled, deveined
14-oz. can artichoke hearts,
   drained, quartered
10-oz. pkg. Green Giant® Rice
   Originals® Frozen Rice
   Medley, thawed
1 tablespoon cornstarch
¼ cup water

In large saucepan or Dutch oven, combine celery, onion, bouillon, oregano, saffron, garlic, 3 cups water and tomatoes; bring to a boil. Reduce heat; cover and simmer 15 minutes or until onion is tender. Add chicken, shrimp, artichoke hearts and rice; bring to a boil. Reduce heat and simmer 3 to 5 minutes or until shrimp turn pink. In small bowl, combine cornstarch and ¼ cup water; mix well. Stir into stew; cook until thickened and bubbly. 6 (1⅓-cup) servings.

NUTRITION INFORMATION PER SERVING

SERVING SIZE: 1-1/3 CUPS		PERCENT U.S. RDA PER SERVING	
CALORIES	200	PROTEIN	35%
PROTEIN	22g	VITAMIN A	10%
CARBOHYDRATE	20g	VITAMIN C	20%
FAT	4g	THIAMINE	10%
CHOLESTEROL	110mg	RIBOFLAVIN	6%
SODIUM	580mg	NIACIN	25%
POTASSIUM	550mg	CALCIUM	8%
		IRON	20%

The cuts of lamb most often used for stews are boneless leg, shoulder, neck and breast. Crunchy vegetables in a sweet-sour sauce round out the flavor in this delicious stew.

Oriental Lamb Stew

1½ to 2 lb. lamb stew meat, cut into 1-inch cubes
1 medium onion, sliced
1 tablespoon oil
1 tablespoon brown sugar
1½ cups apple juice
2 tablespoons soy sauce
2 tablespoons vinegar
10¾-oz. can condensed cream of mushroom soup
1 cup sliced celery
4 carrots, cut into 1-inch pieces
2 tablespoons flour
¼ cup water
2 cups fresh bean sprouts*
8-oz. can sliced water chestnuts, drained
4 cups hot cooked rice

In 5-quart Dutch oven, brown lamb and onion in hot oil. Stir in brown sugar, apple juice, soy sauce, vinegar and mushroom soup. Bring to a boil. Reduce heat; cover and simmer for 45 to 55 minutes or until meat is tender. Stir in celery and carrots. Cover and simmer an additional 30 to 40 minutes or until vegetables are crisp-tender. In small jar with tight-fitting lid, add flour to water; shake well. Stir into stew mixture. Stir in bean sprouts and water chestnuts. Cook over medium heat until mixture thickens and boils, stirring frequently. Serve over rice. 8 servings.

TIPS: *One 16-oz. can bean sprouts, well rinsed, drained, can be substituted for fresh bean sprouts.

Skim fat from surface before serving.

NUTRITION INFORMATION PER SERVING
SERVING SIZE: PERCENT U.S. RDA
1/8 OF RECIPE   PER SERVING

CALORIES	360	PROTEIN	35%
PROTEIN	24g	VITAMIN A	200%
CARBOHYDRATE	49g	VITAMIN C	10%
FAT	7g	THIAMINE	25%
CHOLESTEROL	70mg	RIBOFLAVIN	20%
SODIUM	620mg	NIACIN	30%
POTASSIUM	670mg	CALCIUM	4%
		IRON	20%

Have the party at your house and take advantage of the ease and convenience of this slow cooker chili. Team it up with Cornmeal Sesame Batter Rolls (see Index).

Six-Can Slow Cooker Chili

¼ cup cornmeal
1 teaspoon paprika
½ cup prepared barbecue sauce
28-oz. can (3 cups) tomatoes, undrained, cut up
2 (15-oz.) cans chili without beans
15.5-oz. can pinto beans, undrained, or 15.5-oz. can kidney beans, undrained
15-oz. can caliente-style chili beans, undrained
10.5-oz. can condensed French onion soup

In slow cooker, combine all ingredients; mix well. Cook on high setting for 2 to 4 hours to allow flavors to blend. Or, cook 1 hour on high setting; reduce heat to low setting and cook for 8 to 9 hours. (If slow cooker has 3 settings, use high setting for 1 hour and medium setting for 8 to 9 hours.) Garnish as desired. 8 (1½-cup) servings.

TIP: For hotter chili flavor, 2 teaspoons chili powder can be added.

NUTRITION INFORMATION PER SERVING
SERVING SIZE: PERCENT U.S. RDA
1-1/2 CUPS   PER SERVING

CALORIES	370	PROTEIN	30%
PROTEIN	19g	VITAMIN A	25%
CARBOHYDRATE	34g	VITAMIN C	20%
FAT	18g	THIAMINE	10%
CHOLESTEROL	30mg	RIBOFLAVIN	15%
SODIUM	1640mg	NIACIN	20%
POTASSIUM	830mg	CALCIUM	10%
		IRON	25%

If you are concerned about the level of fat in your diet, we recommend skinning the chicken before preparing this stew.

Oven Chicken Stew

1 teaspoon salt
½ teaspoon poultry
    seasoning
½ teaspoon paprika
¼ teaspoon pepper
2½ to 3-lb. frying chicken, cut into
    8 pieces
2 tablespoons oil
2 tablespoons tomato
    paste
1 cup chicken broth
3 medium carrots, cut in
    half crosswise,
    quartered lengthwise
16-oz. pkg. frozen small
    onions*
6-oz. jar Green Giant® Whole
    Mushrooms, drained
9-oz. pkg. Green Giant®
    Harvest Fresh®
    Frozen Sweet Peas,
    thawed
3 tablespoons
    cornstarch
¼ cup water
    Salt

Heat oven to 350°F. In small bowl, combine 1 teaspoon salt, poultry seasoning, paprika and pepper; mix well. Rub onto chicken. In 5-quart Dutch oven, brown chicken in hot oil over medium-high heat. Remove chicken; drain oil. Add tomato paste to Dutch oven; stir in chicken broth. Bring to a boil. Return chicken to Dutch oven. Stir in carrots, onions and mushrooms; cover. Bake at 350°F. for 1½ hours or until chicken is tender. Stir in peas. Return to stovetop over medium-high heat. In small bowl, combine cornstarch and water. Stir into stew; cook until mixture thickens and boils, stirring frequently. Season to taste with salt. 6 (1⅓-cup) servings.

Pictured left to right: Cornmeal Breadsticks p. 72, Oven Chicken Stew

TIPS: *A 16-oz. jar small onions, drained, can be substituted for frozen onions; add with peas.

Remaining tomato paste can be frozen for later use.

NUTRITION INFORMATION PER SERVING

SERVING SIZE: 1-1/3 CUPS		PERCENT U.S. RDA PER SERVING	
CALORIES	270	PROTEIN	40%
PROTEIN	25g	VITAMIN A	210%
CARBOHYDRATE	21g	VITAMIN C	20%
FAT	10g	THIAMINE	10%
CHOLESTEROL	60mg	RIBOFLAVIN	15%
SODIUM	875mg	NIACIN	40%
POTASSIUM	530mg	CALCIUM	4%
		IRON	10%

Cook's Note

Tips for Reducing Salt

We have consciously used a minimum amount of salt in all of our recipes. Generally, processed foods have salt already added so if available, purchase reduced-sodium ingredients such as canned broths, condensed soups and tomatoes. When using canned broth, bouillon cubes or instant bouillon diluted in water, we suggest waiting to add salt to taste until after all ingredients are combined to avoid over salting.

With ingredients on hand, it will take only 10 minutes to prepare this tasty bean and pasta stew.

🌀 Garbanzo Bean Stew

1	cup water
15-oz.	can tomato sauce
15-oz.	can garbanzo beans, undrained
14½-oz.	can (1½ cups) salad tomato wedges, undrained
3-oz.	pkg. oriental noodles with beef flavor packet
1	cup Green Giant® Frozen Cut Leaf Spinach (from 16-oz. pkg.), thawed, or coarsely chopped fresh spinach
1	cup chopped, cooked ham, if desired

In medium saucepan, combine 1 cup water, tomato sauce, beans and tomatoes. Bring to a boil. Break oriental noodles into quarters; stir into bean mixture. Cook 2 minutes. Remove from heat. Stir in contents of beef flavor packet, spinach and ham. Let stand covered 2 to 3 minutes or until thoroughly heated. 5 (1¼-cup) servings.

🔲 MICROWAVE DIRECTIONS: In 3-quart microwave-safe casserole, combine 1 cup water, tomato sauce, beans and tomatoes; cover tightly. Microwave on HIGH for 9 to 10 minutes or until mixture boils, stirring once halfway through cooking. Break oriental noodles into quarters; stir into bean mixture. Microwave uncovered on HIGH for 2 minutes, stirring once halfway through cooking. Stir in contents of beef flavor packet, spinach and ham. Let stand covered 3 to 5 minutes or until thoroughly heated.

NUTRITION INFORMATION PER SERVING

SERVING SIZE: 1-1/4 CUPS		PERCENT U.S. RDA PER SERVING	
CALORIES	270	PROTEIN	25%
PROTEIN	16g	VITAMIN A	100%
CARBOHYDRATE	33g	VITAMIN C	50%
FAT	10g	THIAMINE	30%
CHOLESTEROL	30mg	RIBOFLAVIN	20%
SODIUM	1930mg	NIACIN	20%
POTASSIUM	1040mg	CALCIUM	10%
		IRON	35%

Pictured top to bottom: Microwave Corn Bread p. 70, Garbanzo Bean Stew

What makes Texas-style chili unique is its chunks of meat and lack of beans. The Texans include chile peppers instead of chili powder! We've gone a step farther and included some wonderful corn bread dumplings to complete this outstanding chili.

Texas-Style Chili with Corn Bread Dumplings

CHILI

2½	lb. beef round steak, trimmed, cut into ½-inch cubes
3	tablespoons oil
1	cup chopped onions
2	garlic cloves, finely chopped
1	tablespoon cumin
1	tablespoon oregano leaves
½	teaspoon paprika
¼ to ½	teaspoon cinnamon
16-oz.	can (2 cups) tomatoes, undrained, cut up
15-oz.	can tomato sauce
12-oz.	can beer or 1½ cups beef broth
2	serrano chile peppers, seeded, finely chopped
2	jalapeño chile peppers, seeded, finely chopped

DUMPLINGS

½	cup Pillsbury's BEST® All Purpose or Unbleached Flour
¾	cup cornmeal
2	teaspoons baking powder
½	teaspoon salt
½	cup milk
1	tablespoon oil

In 5-quart Dutch oven, brown meat in oil with onion, garlic, cumin, oregano, paprika and cinnamon. Stir in remaining chili ingredients. Bring to a boil. Reduce heat and simmer 1¼ hours or until meat is tender.

To prepare dumplings, lightly spoon flour into measuring cup; level off. In medium bowl, combine flour, cornmeal, baking powder and salt; blend well. Add milk and oil; stir just until dry ingredients are moistened. Bring chili to a boil. Drop dumpling dough by rounded tablespoonfuls onto bubbling chili. Reduce heat; cover tightly and simmer 15 minutes or until dumplings are fluffy and no longer doughy. 10 (1-cup) servings.

HIGH ALTITUDE – Above 3500 Feet: No change.

NUTRITION INFORMATION PER SERVING

SERVING SIZE: 1 CUP		PERCENT U.S. RDA PER SERVING	
CALORIES	320	PROTEIN	45%
PROTEIN	29g	VITAMIN A	60%
CARBOHYDRATE	22g	VITAMIN C	70%
FAT	11g	THIAMINE	15%
CHOLESTEROL	70mg	RIBOFLAVIN	20%
SODIUM	560mg	NIACIN	35%
POTASSIUM	780mg	CALCIUM	10%
		IRON	25%

Cook's Note

Chile Pepper Handling Tips

As members of the capsicum genus, chile peppers contain the colorless irritant capsaicin, which gives peppers their characteristic hot bite. Direct contact with capsaicin can irritate the skin and eyes. Wear rubber gloves when chopping fresh jalapeno, serrano or other varieties of chile peppers and avoid touching your eyes. Scrub knife and cutting board when finished.

Texas-Style Chili with Corn Bread Dumplings

Regional
Specialties

Regional Specialties

North, South, East, West — each region around the U.S.A. creates its own soups and stews best.

From California to New York, from the northern forests to the Gulf, each region of the United States has developed soups and stews that define it, that reflect its ethnic heritage and traditions, and that use the very best locally available ingredients.

In this chapter, there are recipes from five regions:

- Northeast — Maine to Maryland.
- South — West Virginia to the Gulf Coast states.
- Southwest — From south of the Great Plains to the Rio Grande.
- Mid-America — Great Lakes and Great Plains states.
- Northwest — Pacific Northwest and the mountain states.

The famous seafood, vegetable and poultry chowders of the Northeast trace their roots to North Atlantic villages where fisherfolk contributed a portion of the day's catch to the community iron kettle called "la chaudiere."

Southern love of neighborly gatherings has created two delectable dishes, burgoos and gumbos. Burgoo is a traditional favorite served in Kentucky during Derby Days. Gumbo blends the cookery of France and Spain with the exotic spice and flair of the Deep South.

The influences of the Conquistidors and Aztecs can still be found in popular Southwestern fare. Zesty seasonings characterize tempting dishes like *Southwestern Black Bean Soup* served with warm tortillas and cool guacamole.

Fish from lakes and streams, wild rice harvested from Northern waters and the grains and vegetables from Midwestern farms make the soups and stews of Mid-America hearty and satisfying.

Salmon, clams and a cornucopia of fruits and vegetables, combine in a symphony of flavors in favorite Pacific Northwest dishes such as *Oregon Beef-Fruit Stew* and *Salmon 'n Vegetable Chowder.*

Pictured on previous page: Salmon 'n Vegetable Chowder

Chowders are typically thought of as East coast fare, but in this recipe Idaho potatoes and Pacific salmon combine for a Northwestern version.

Salmon 'n Vegetable Chowder

        1 cup diced, peeled potatoes
      ¼ cup chopped onion
      ¼ cup water
        2 tablespoons flour
      ⅛ teaspoon salt
      ⅛ teaspoon white pepper
        2 cups milk
  9-oz. pkg. Green Giant® Broccoli, Cauliflower and Carrots Frozen in Butter Sauce, thawed*
  6½-oz. can salmon, drained, chunked
          Chopped fresh dill weed

🖾 MICROWAVE DIRECTIONS: In 2-quart microwave-safe casserole, combine potatoes, onion and water; cover tightly. Microwave on HIGH for 4 to 6 minutes or until potatoes are tender, stirring once halfway through cooking. In small bowl, combine flour, salt and white pepper; blend well. Gradually stir in milk. Stir milk mixture into potato mixture. Add vegetable mixture; mix well. Cover tightly. Microwave on HIGH for 7 to 9 minutes or until bubbly and vegetables are crisp-tender, stirring twice during cooking. Stir in salmon. Microwave on HIGH for 1 minute or until thoroughly heated. Garnish each serving with dill weed. 3 (1½-cup) servings.

CONVENTIONAL DIRECTIONS: In medium saucepan, combine potatoes, onion and water. Bring to a boil. Reduce heat; cover and simmer 8 to 10 minutes or until potatoes are tender. In small bowl, combine flour, salt and white pepper; blend well. Gradually stir in milk. Stir milk mixture into potato mixture. Cook until mixture is hot, stirring constantly. Add vegetable mixture; cover and simmer until vegetables are crisp-tender, about 10 minutes, stirring occasionally. Add salmon; heat gently until thoroughly heated. Garnish each serving with dill weed.

TIP: *A 10-oz. pkg. of Green Giant® Broccoli, Cauliflower and Carrots Frozen in a Cheese Flavored Sauce can be substituted for vegetables in butter sauce.

NUTRITION INFORMATION PER SERVING

SERVING SIZE: 1-1/2 CUPS		PERCENT U.S. RDA PER SERVING	
CALORIES	250	PROTEIN	30%
PROTEIN	19g	VITAMIN A	100%
CARBOHYDRATE	26g	VITAMIN C	60%
FAT	8g	THIAMINE	10%
CHOLESTEROL	35mg	RIBOFLAVIN	25%
SODIUM	680mg	NIACIN	20%
POTASSIUM	870mg	CALCIUM	35%
		IRON	10%

Thanks to the Italian fishermen who settled in San Francisco, we have this fishermen's stew—a combined treasure of fish and shellfish in a tomato base. Cioppino (Cha-pee-no) ingredients vary from day to day depending on the seafood available. This recipe provides a typical mixture of seafood found in Cioppino. It's somewhat messy to eat, but that's half the fun.

Cioppino

28-oz. can (3 cups) tomatoes, undrained, cut up
16-oz. can (2 cups) stewed tomatoes, undrained, cut up
8-oz. can tomato sauce
1 cup sauterne wine, dry white wine or fish broth
2 teaspoons basil leaves
1 teaspoon salt
¼ teaspoon pepper
12 small clams in the shell, washed
⅓ cup oil
1½ cups chopped onions
1 cup chopped fresh parsley
1 lb. fresh medium shrimp, shelled, deveined*
6 garlic cloves, chopped
1 lb. frozen snow or dungeness crab legs in the shell, thawed, cracked
1 lb. fresh halibut or cod, cut into 1½-inch pieces
French bread

In 5-quart Dutch oven, combine tomatoes, stewed tomatoes, tomato sauce, wine, basil, salt and pepper. Bring to a boil. Reduce heat; simmer 10 minutes, stirring occasionally. Return to a boil; add clams. Cover tightly and cook over medium heat 4 to 6 minutes or until clam shells open.

In medium saucepan, heat oil. Stir in onions, parsley, shrimp and garlic. Simmer covered 3 to 5 minutes or until shrimp are light pink, stirring occasionally. Stir shrimp mixture into tomato-clam mixture. Add crab. Simmer uncovered 5 minutes. Add fish pieces. Simmer uncovered an additional 2 to 3 minutes or until fish flakes easily with fork. Serve with thick slices of French bread to dip in rich broth. 6 (1½-cup) servings.

TIP: *One 12-oz. pkg. frozen medium shrimp, cooked, drained, can be substituted for fresh shrimp.

NUTRITION INFORMATION PER SERVING

SERVING SIZE: 1-1/2 CUPS		PERCENT U.S. RDA PER SERVING	
CALORIES	390	PROTEIN	60%
PROTEIN	38g	VITAMIN A	45%
CARBOHYDRATE	20g	VITAMIN C	50%
FAT	16g	THIAMINE	15%
CHOLESTEROL	130mg	RIBOFLAVIN	10%
SODIUM	1370mg	NIACIN	45%
POTASSIUM	1350mg	CALCIUM	20%
		IRON	40%

Meat and dried fruits are simmered in apple cider to create this Northwestern favorite. Our version features beef, but traditional recipes call for venison, elk or antelope.

Oregon Beef-Fruit Stew

2 tablespoons oil
2 lb. beef stew meat, cut into 1-inch cubes
2 cups apple cider
3 small onions, thinly sliced
1 lemon slice
¼ teaspoon allspice
¼ teaspoon pepper
8-oz. pkg. dried mixed fruit

Heat oven to 350°F. Heat oil in 4-quart Dutch oven over medium-high heat; brown beef. Add apple cider; bring to a boil. Remove from heat; add remaining ingredients except dried fruit. Cover. Bake at 350°F. for 1½ hours. Add dried fruit; bake for an additional 20 to 30 minutes or until fruit is soft and meat is tender. Remove lemon slice. 4 (1¼-cup) servings.

NUTRITION INFORMATION PER SERVING

SERVING SIZE: 1-1/4 CUPS		PERCENT U.S. RDA PER SERVING	
CALORIES	570	PROTEIN	80%
PROTEIN	52g	VITAMIN A	15%
CARBOHYDRATE	52g	VITAMIN C	6%
FAT	17g	THIAMINE	15%
CHOLESTEROL	130mg	RIBOFLAVIN	25%
SODIUM	110mg	NIACIN	50%
POTASSIUM	1390mg	CALCIUM	2%
		IRON	35%

Potato fields dominate eastern Washington, southern Idaho and eastern Oregon. It's not surprising, therefore, that Northwesterners enjoy potato soup.

Quick Potato Onion Soup

1 cup finely chopped onions or sliced leeks
1 cup sliced carrots
¾ cup sliced celery
¼ cup margarine or butter
3 cups milk
2 cups half-and-half
1 cup Hungry Jack® Mashed Potato Flakes
¾ teaspoon salt
½ to ¾ teaspoon pepper
2 to 3 drops hot pepper sauce
Chopped fresh parsley, shredded cheese or croutons, if desired

In large saucepan over medium heat, cook onions, carrots and celery in margarine for 5 minutes or until crisp-tender. Add milk and half-and-half; bring to a boil. Reduce heat; simmer 10 minutes, stirring occasionally. Stir in potato flakes, salt, pepper and hot pepper sauce. Simmer 5 minutes, stirring constantly. Garnish with chopped parsley, shredded cheese or croutons. Serve immediately. 4 (1½-cup) servings.

NUTRITION INFORMATION PER SERVING

SERVING SIZE: 1-1/2 CUPS		PERCENT U.S. RDA PER SERVING	
CALORIES	440	PROTEIN	20%
PROTEIN	12g	VITAMIN A	200%
CARBOHYDRATE	33g	VITAMIN C	15%
FAT	29g	THIAMINE	10%
CHOLESTEROL	60mg	RIBOFLAVIN	35%
SODIUM	730mg	NIACIN	6%
POTASSIUM	900mg	CALCIUM	40%
		IRON	4%

This Mexican-inspired tomato soup is served in the Southwest as a starter soup. It is topped with a garnish of toasted flour tortilla strips. However, corn tortillas can be substituted for a crunchy variation.

Zesty Tortilla Soup

4 (8-inch)	flour tortillas
1	cup diced onions
2	garlic cloves, finely chopped
2	tablespoons oil
1	teaspoon cumin
48-oz.	can (6 cups) spicy hot cocktail vegetable juice
14½-oz.	can (1½ cups) whole tomatoes, seeded, chopped, undrained
14½-oz.	can chicken broth
½	cup thinly sliced green onions
4	oz. (1 cup) shredded Monterey jack cheese
	Fresh cilantro, if desired

Heat oven to 375°F. Stack tortillas and cut into ½-inch wide strips. Place in single layer on ungreased cookie sheet. Bake at 375°F. for 15 minutes or until crisp and toasted. Set aside.

Continued on p. 50

Pictured top to bottom: Microwave Corn Bread (blue cornmeal) p. 70, Southwestern Black Bean Soup p. 50, Zesty Tortilla Soup

Continued from p. 49

In large saucepan, cook onions and garlic in oil until translucent. Add cumin, vegetable juice, tomatoes and chicken broth. Bring to a boil. Reduce heat; simmer 20 minutes to blend flavors. Divide green onions and cheese evenly among 9 soup bowls. Ladle 1 cup soup over onions and cheese. Top with tortilla strips. Garnish with sprigs of fresh cilantro. 9 (1-cup) servings.

TIP: For hotter, spicier flavor, add ½ teaspoon chili powder with cumin.

NUTRITION INFORMATION PER SERVING

SERVING SIZE: 1 CUP		PERCENT U.S. RDA PER SERVING	
CALORIES	200	PROTEIN	10%
PROTEIN	7g	VITAMIN A	50%
CARBOHYDRATE	22g	VITAMIN C	70%
FAT	9g	THIAMINE	10%
CHOLESTEROL	10mg	RIBOFLAVIN	10%
SODIUM	990mg	NIACIN	15%
POTASSIUM	540mg	CALCIUM	15%
		IRON	10%

The rich cultural heritage of the Southwest is reflected in this colorful soup. It is especially delicious when served with warm flour tortillas spread with guacamole or avocado butter.

Southwestern Black Bean Soup

- 16 oz. (2¼ cups) black turtle beans
- 6 cups water
- 2 (10½-oz.) cans condensed beef broth
- 2 cans water
- 1 large carrot, shredded
- 2 tablespoons taco seasoning mix
- 1 lb. chorizo sausage or hot Italian sausage in casings
- 2 (14½-oz.) cans (2 cups) stewed tomatoes
- 12-oz. can Green Giant® Mexicorn® Whole Kernel Corn with Green and Red Sweet Peppers, undrained

TOPPING

- ⅓ cup plain lowfat yogurt
- 3 tablespoons dairy sour cream
- 1 green onion, finely chopped

Sort beans. Rinse well; drain. In 6-quart Dutch oven, combine beans and 6 cups water. Bring to a boil. Boil 2 minutes; remove from heat. Cover and let stand 1 hour.* Drain beans. Add beef broth, 2 cans water, carrot and taco seasoning. Bring to a boil. Reduce heat; cover and simmer until beans are tender but not mushy, about 30 minutes.** Meanwhile, pierce chorizo. Brown sausage in large heavy skillet over medium heat, turning often, about 15 minutes. Drain on paper towel; cut into thin slices. Add to soup along with stewed tomatoes and corn; stir. Cover partially; simmer 30 minutes.

In small bowl, combine all topping ingredients; mix well. Pour soup into serving bowls. Spoon 1 tablespoon topping over each serving. 8 (1½-cup) servings.

TIPS: *An alternative method for hydrating the beans is soaking them in water overnight.

**Soup can be prepared to this point and frozen up to 1 month.

NUTRITION INFORMATION PER SERVING

SERVING SIZE: 1-1/2 CUPS		PERCENT U.S. RDA PER SERVING	
CALORIES	410	PROTEIN	35%
PROTEIN	24g	VITAMIN A	90%
CARBOHYDRATE	59g	VITAMIN C	8%
FAT	9g	THIAMINE	50%
CHOLESTEROL	25mg	RIBOFLAVIN	20%
SODIUM	1000mg	NIACIN	20%
POTASSIUM	1300mg	CALCIUM	15%
		IRON	35%

Lean turkey is quickly stewed in a spicy tomato sauce. Cornmeal, used to thicken the stew, is a common ingredient in Southwestern cuisine.

Tex-Mex Turkey Stew

- 2 tablespoons oil
- 2 lb. fresh turkey tenderloins or breast roast, cut into 2 by ½-inch strips
- 1 cup coarsely chopped onions
- 1 teaspoon oregano leaves
- 1 teaspoon cumin
- 1 teaspoon chicken-flavor instant bouillon or 1 chicken-flavor bouillon cube
- 1 cup water
- 1 cup picante sauce
- 14½-oz. can (1½ cups) tomato wedges, undrained
- ⅓ cup cornmeal
- ½ teaspoon salt
- ¼ teaspoon pepper
- 1 green bell pepper, cut into ¾-inch chunks
- 2½-oz. jar (1 cup) pitted green olives, drained

Heat oil in 4 to 6-quart Dutch oven over medium-high heat; brown turkey. Drain. Add onions, oregano, cumin, bouillon, water, picante sauce and tomatoes. Bring to a boil. Reduce heat; cover and simmer 18 to 25 minutes or until turkey is tender.

In small bowl, combine cornmeal, salt and pepper; mix well. Slowly stir into stew. Stir in green pepper and olives; cook uncovered until green pepper is crisp-tender, about 5 minutes. 4 (1½-cup) servings.

NUTRITION INFORMATION PER SERVING

SERVING SIZE: 1-1/2 CUPS		PERCENT U.S. RDA PER SERVING	
CALORIES	310	PROTEIN	70%
PROTEIN	45g	VITAMIN A	15%
CARBOHYDRATE	14g	VITAMIN C	35%
FAT	8g	THIAMINE	10%
CHOLESTEROL	120mg	RIBOFLAVIN	15%
SODIUM	1020mg	NIACIN	60%
POTASSIUM	770mg	CALCIUM	6%
		IRON	20%

Chile peppers and dried beans are characteristic of Southwestern cuisine.

Pueblo Meatball Stew

- 1 lb. ground beef
- 1 egg, slightly beaten
- ¼ teaspoon salt
- ¼ teaspoon pepper
- 1 tablespoon oil
- 1 cup water
- 1 beef-flavor bouillon cube or 1 teaspoon beef-flavor instant bouillon
- 10¾-oz. can condensed tomato soup
- 1 tablespoon chili powder
- 1 teaspoon oregano leaves
- 2 cups sliced yellow or zucchini squash, cut into ½-inch slices
- 1 green bell pepper, cut into ½-inch strips
- 2 large onions, sliced
- 17-oz. can Green Giant® Whole Kernel Golden Sweet Corn, drained
- 15.5-oz. can pinto beans, drained

In large bowl, combine ground beef, egg, salt and pepper; mix well. Shape ground beef mixture into twelve 1½-inch balls. Heat oil in Dutch oven over medium heat; brown meatballs. Drain.

In small saucepan, bring water to a boil; dissolve bouillon cube. Stir in soup, chili powder and oregano. Add soup mixture to meatballs. Bring to a boil. Cover; simmer 15 minutes. Add squash, green pepper, onions, corn and beans. Cover; simmer 10 to 15 minutes or until vegetables are crisp-tender, stirring occasionally. 5 (1½-cup) servings.

NUTRITION INFORMATION PER SERVING

SERVING SIZE: 1-1/2 CUPS		PERCENT U.S. RDA PER SERVING	
CALORIES	450	PROTEIN	40%
PROTEIN	25g	VITAMIN A	30%
CARBOHYDRATE	47g	VITAMIN C	80%
FAT	18g	THIAMINE	20%
CHOLESTEROL	110mg	RIBOFLAVIN	20%
SODIUM	970mg	NIACIN	25%
POTASSIUM	1010mg	CALCIUM	8%
		IRON	30%

MID-AMERICA

The Heartland is truly the bread basket of America, where corn and grain cover the land and beef and pork fill the dinner table. This hearty stew with its distinctive pioneer flavor is a good example of a "comfort food" from this area.

Chuck Wagon Stew with Dill Dumplings

STEW

1½ lb. boneless lean beef chuck roast, cut into 1-inch cubes
Flour
½ cup chopped onion
1 tablespoon oil
16-oz. can (2 cups) whole tomatoes, undrained, cut up
¾ cup beef broth
3 small potatoes, peeled, cut into 1-inch pieces
2 large carrots, cut into 1-inch pieces
15½-oz. can red kidney beans, undrained
2 to 3 teaspoons Worcestershire sauce
Salt
Pepper
¼ cup flour
½ cup cold water

DUMPLINGS

1½ cups Hungry Jack® Buttermilk, Extra Lights® or Complete Pancake Mix
2 teaspoons dill weed
½ cup milk

Coat beef cubes lightly with flour. In large saucepan, brown beef and onion in oil. Add tomatoes and beef broth; mix well. Bring to a boil. Reduce heat; cover and simmer 45 minutes or until beef is just tender. Stir in potatoes and carrots; cover and simmer an additional 20 to 30 minutes or until vegetables are tender. Stir in beans and Worcestershire sauce; add salt and pepper to taste. In small jar with tight-fitting lid, add ¼ cup flour to cold water; shake well. Stir into stew mixture. Cook over medium heat until mixture boils and thickens, stirring constantly.

In medium bowl, combine dumpling ingredients; blend well. Drop dumpling dough by rounded tablespoonfuls onto boiling stew mixture. Reduce heat; simmer 10 minutes. Cover and simmer an additional 10 minutes or until dumplings are fluffy and no longer doughy. 4 to 6 servings.

HIGH ALTITUDE—Above 3500 Feet: No change.

NUTRITION INFORMATION PER SERVING

SERVING SIZE: 1/6 OF RECIPE		PERCENT U.S. RDA PER SERVING	
CALORIES	520	PROTEIN	60%
PROTEIN	37g	VITAMIN A	220%
CARBOHYDRATE	68g	VITAMIN C	30%
FAT	11g	THIAMINE	35%
CHOLESTEROL	80mg	RIBOFLAVIN	30%
SODIUM	850mg	NIACIN	35%
POTASSIUM	1070mg	CALCIUM	10%
		IRON	40%

At one time, the only source of wild rice was the Indians in Northern Minnesota. Now it comes conveniently in Rice Originals® to make wonderful low fat wild rice soup in short order.

Microwave White 'n Wild Rice Soup

10-oz.	pkg. Green Giant® Rice Originals® Frozen Long Grain White and Wild Rice
2	tablespoons reduced-calorie or regular margarine or butter
½	cup sliced fresh mushrooms or 2.5-oz. jar Green Giant® Sliced Mushrooms, drained
¼	cup finely chopped onion
¼	cup flour
2	cups chicken broth
12-oz.	can evaporated skim milk or 1½ cups half-and-half
2	tablespoons sherry, if desired
	Chopped fresh parsley

🖾 MICROWAVE DIRECTIONS:
Microwave rice mixture according to package microwave directions; set aside. In 3-quart microwave-safe bowl, combine margarine, mushrooms and onion. Cover tightly; microwave on HIGH for 1½ to 2 minutes or until tender. Stir in flour; gradually stir in broth. Cover tightly; microwave on HIGH for 6 to 8 minutes or until slightly thickened and bubbly, stirring twice during cooking. Stir in evaporated skim milk and rice mixture; cover tightly. Microwave on HIGH for 2 to 3 minutes or until thoroughly heated. Stir in sherry. Garnish with parsley. 5 (1-cup) servings.

CONVENTIONAL DIRECTIONS:
Prepare rice mixture according to package directions; set aside. Meanwhile, melt margarine in large saucepan over medium heat. Cook mushrooms and onion in margarine until tender. Stir in flour; heat until bubbly, stirring constantly. Gradually stir in broth. Bring to a boil; reduce heat. Stir in evaporated skim milk and rice mixture. Cook until thoroughly heated. Stir in sherry. Garnish with parsley.

NUTRITION INFORMATION PER SERVING

SERVING SIZE: 1 CUP		PERCENT U.S. RDA PER SERVING	
CALORIES	180	PROTEIN	10%
PROTEIN	8g	VITAMIN A	10%
CARBOHYDRATE	27g	VITAMIN C	4%
FAT	4g	THIAMINE	10%
CHOLESTEROL	2mg	RIBOFLAVIN	20%
SODIUM	580mg	NIACIN	6%
POTASSIUM	330mg	CALCIUM	25%
		IRON	8%

Old-Fashioned Vegetable Soup

2 to 3 lb. meaty beef bones, such as shank, cut into 3-inch pieces
6 to 8 cups water*
2 beef-flavor bouillon cubes or 2 teaspoons instant beef-flavor bouillon
1½ teaspoons salt
¼ teaspoon thyme leaves or marjoram leaves
6 peppercorns or ¼ teaspoon pepper
2 whole allspice
1 bay leaf
2 cups cubed, peeled potatoes
1 cup sliced celery
1 cup sliced carrots
½ cup chopped onion
16-oz. can (2 cups) tomatoes, undrained, cut up
11-oz. can Green Giant® Niblets® Whole Kernel Golden Sweet Corn

In 5-quart Dutch oven, combine beef bones and water. Bring to a boil. Reduce heat; cover and simmer 30 minutes. Skim off any residue that rises to the surface. Add bouillon cubes, salt, thyme, peppercorns, allspice and bay leaf. Simmer covered an additional 2½ to 3 hours or until meat is tender. Remove meat, peppercorns, allspice and bay leaf from broth. Remove meat from bones; cut into bite-sized pieces. Skim fat from broth. Return meat to broth. Stir in remaining ingredients. Bring to a boil. Reduce heat; cover and simmer 30 minutes or until vegetables are tender. 8 (1½-cup) servings.

NUTRITION INFORMATION PER SERVING

SERVING SIZE: 1-1/2 CUPS		PERCENT U.S. RDA PER SERVING	
CALORIES	220	PROTEIN	40%
PROTEIN	26g	VITAMIN A	90%
CARBOHYDRATE	18g	VITAMIN C	25%
FAT	5g	THIAMINE	10%
CHOLESTEROL	60mg	RIBOFLAVIN	10%
SODIUM	870mg	NIACIN	30%
POTASSIUM	820mg	CALCIUM	6%
		IRON	20%

Serve this stew with plates on the side for the corn-on-the-cob.

Midwestern Fish Stew

¼ lb. lean bacon, diced
1 cup sliced onions
2 cups fish broth or chicken broth
2 cups dry white wine or water
16-oz. can (2 cups) tomatoes, undrained, cut up
1 lb. new red potatoes, quartered
½ cup minced fresh parsley
2 teaspoons minced fresh tarragon or 1 teaspoon tarragon leaves
2 teaspoons minced fresh thyme or 1 teaspoon thyme leaves
¼ teaspoon pepper
1 cup julienne red bell pepper
1 cup Green Giant® Frozen Cut Green Beans (from 16-oz. pkg.)
6 Green Giant® Nibblers® Frozen Corn-on-the-Cob
1½ lb. boneless, skinless fish, cut into 1-inch chunks
Salt

In 6-quart Dutch oven, cook bacon until almost crisp. Add onions; cook until tender. Drain fat. Add fish broth, wine, tomatoes, potatoes, parsley, tarragon, thyme and pepper. Bring to a boil. Reduce heat; simmer, partially covered, 20 to 25 minutes or until potatoes are almost tender. Add red pepper, green beans, corn and fish. Bring to a boil. Simmer covered 7 to 9 minutes or until fish flakes easily with a fork. Season to taste with salt. 6 (2-cup) servings.

NUTRITION INFORMATION PER SERVING

SERVING SIZE: 2 CUPS		PERCENT U.S. RDA PER SERVING	
CALORIES	360	PROTEIN	40%
PROTEIN	27g	VITAMIN A	40%
CARBOHYDRATE	40g	VITAMIN C	80%
FAT	4g	THIAMINE	20%
CHOLESTEROL	50mg	RIBOFLAVIN	15%
SODIUM	530mg	NIACIN	30%
POTASSIUM	1340mg	CALCIUM	8%
		IRON	15%

Midwestern Fish Stew

NORTHEAST

NUTRITION INFORMATION PER SERVING

SERVING SIZE: 1/5 OF RECIPE		PERCENT U.S. RDA PER SERVING	
CALORIES	340	PROTEIN	35%
PROTEIN	22g	VITAMIN A	330%
CARBOHYDRATE	23g	VITAMIN C	20%
FAT	18g	THIAMINE	10%
CHOLESTEROL	120mg	RIBOFLAVIN	20%
SODIUM	1130mg	NIACIN	30%
POTASSIUM	610mg	CALCIUM	8%
		IRON	10%

Chowders are associated with New England. An authentic American chowder usually contains shellfish or fish, salt pork or bacon, vegetables, and milk or broth.

The ground turkey featured in this stew can be found in the fresh or frozen meat section of your supermarket.

Hearty Meatball Stew

1 lb. ground turkey
1 egg
¼ cup chopped onion
½ teaspoon garlic salt
¼ teaspoon pepper
1 tablespoon oil
1 beef-flavor bouillon cube or 1 teaspoon beef-flavor instant bouillon
1½ cups boiling water
10¾-oz. can condensed golden mushroom soup
4 carrots, cut into ½-inch pieces
3 celery stalks, cut into ½-inch pieces
1 medium onion, sliced
11-oz. can Green Giant® Niblets® Whole Kernel Golden Sweet Corn

In medium bowl, combine ground turkey, egg, onion, garlic salt and pepper; mix well. Shape into 1½-inch balls. In Dutch oven, brown meatballs in hot oil; drain. Dissolve bouillon in boiling water. Add bouillon mixture and remaining ingredients to meatballs; stir gently. Cover; bring to a boil. Reduce heat; simmer 25 to 30 minutes or until vegetables are tender.
4 to 5 servings.

Boston-Style Fish Chowder

4 slices bacon, diced
½ cup chopped celery
1 pkg. Pillsbury Creamy White Sauce Scalloped Potatoes
3½ cups milk
2 cups water
2 tablespoons chopped fresh parsley or 1 tablespoon parsley flakes
¼ teaspoon fresh ground pepper
1 lb. white fish fillets, cut into 1-inch pieces*

In large saucepan, cook bacon until crisp. Remove from pan; drain on paper towels. Set aside. Drain bacon drippings, reserving 1 tablespoon. Cook celery in reserved bacon drippings until crisp-tender. Add scalloped potatoes with contents of sauce mix envelope, milk, water, parsley and pepper; stir well. Bring to a boil; reduce heat. Cover; simmer 15 minutes, stirring occasionally. Stir in fish; cook an additional 10 minutes or until fish flakes easily with fork, stirring occasionally. Garnish with bacon.
4 (1½-cup) servings.

TIP: *Examples of white fish are sole, perch, cod, halibut and walleye.

NUTRITION INFORMATION PER SERVING

SERVING SIZE: 1-1/2 CUPS		PERCENT U.S. RDA PER SERVING	
CALORIES	370	PROTEIN	50%
PROTEIN	33g	VITAMIN A	10%
CARBOHYDRATE	39g	VITAMIN C	10%
FAT	8g	THIAMINE	15%
CHOLESTEROL	70mg	RIBOFLAVIN	35%
SODIUM	860mg	NIACIN	25%
POTASSIUM	1180mg	CALCIUM	35%
		IRON	8%

Crab surimi, cheese and leeks combine to flavor a rich soup of New England heritage.

Yankee Cream Cheese Soup

½ cup margarine or butter
6 large leeks, white part only, finely chopped, or 6 small onions, finely chopped
½ cup Pillsbury's BEST® All Purpose or Unbleached Flour
4 cups fish or chicken broth
1 cup plain yogurt
8-oz. pkg. cream cheese, softened*
2 egg yolks
¼ cup diced red bell pepper or 2½-oz. jar chopped pimento, drained
6-oz. pkg. crab surimi or crabmeat
Salt

Melt margarine in large saucepan or Dutch oven over medium heat. Cook leeks until translucent, stirring frequently, about 5 minutes. Lightly spoon flour into measuring cup; level off. Stir in flour; cook until bubbly. Gradually stir in fish broth. Bring to a boil. Reduce heat; simmer 10 minutes, stirring occasionally. Remove from heat.

In food processor bowl with metal blade or blender container, puree leek mixture. (Process in batches if necessary.) Return to saucepan. In same processor bowl, process yogurt, cream cheese and egg yolks with on-off pulses until blended.

Add 2 cups of the leek mixture through feed tube to cheese mixture. Process just to blend. Stir into remaining leek mixture. Stir in red pepper and crab. Cook over medium-low heat for 10 to 15 minutes or until thoroughly heated, stirring occasionally. DO NOT BOIL. Season to taste with salt. Garnish as desired.
10 (1-cup) servings.

TIP: *An 8-oz. pkg. of light cream cheese or Neufchatel cheese can be substituted for cream cheese.

NUTRITION INFORMATION PER SERVING

SERVING SIZE: 1 CUP		PERCENT U.S. RDA PER SERVING	
CALORIES	240	PROTEIN	10%
PROTEIN	7g	VITAMIN A	20%
CARBOHYDRATE	10g	VITAMIN C	6%
FAT	19g	THIAMINE	4%
CHOLESTEROL	90mg	RIBOFLAVIN	8%
SODIUM	340mg	NIACIN	2%
POTASSIUM	140mg	CALCIUM	8%
		IRON	6%

Cook's Note

Quick Chicken or Beef Broth

When a recipe calls for chicken or beef broth you can make your own or use convenience products. These substitutes will be saltier than homemade broth. Therefore, when using one of these substitutes, we suggest you combine all ingredients before adding salt to taste.

• A 14½-oz. can of beef or chicken broth equals about 1¾ cups broth.

• A 10½-oz. can of condensed beef broth or 10¾-oz. can of condensed chicken broth diluted with 1 soup can of water equals 2⅔ cups broth.

• One beef- or chicken-flavored bouillon cube, or 1 teaspoon instant beef or chicken flavor instant bouillon diluted with 1 cup water equals 1 cup broth.

A bisque is a thick cream soup. A true Northeasterner would use whipping cream to make this recipe. This version is a health conscious variation that captures the rich taste and at the same time reduces the levels of fat and salt.

Chesapeake Oyster Bisque

- 1 pint fresh oysters or 2 (8-oz.) cans oysters, drained, reserving liquid
- ¼ cup thinly sliced celery
- ¼ cup finely chopped onion
- 2 tablespoons reduced-calorie margarine
- 3 tablespoons flour
- ¼ teaspoon salt
- ¼ teaspoon white pepper
- 2 cups skim milk
- 12-oz. can evaporated skim milk
- 2 tablespoons snipped fresh chives

Chop oysters; set aside. In medium saucepan, cook celery and onion in margarine until tender. Stir in flour, salt and white pepper. Cook over low heat 1 minute, stirring constantly. Gradually stir in skim milk and evaporated milk until smooth. Cook over low heat 5 to 10 minutes or until slightly thickened, stirring constantly. DO NOT BOIL. Add oysters, reserved liquid and chives. Heat over low heat until thoroughly heated, stirring frequently. 4 (1½-cup) servings.

NUTRITION INFORMATION PER SERVING

SERVING SIZE: 1-1/2 CUPS		PERCENT U.S. RDA PER SERVING	
CALORIES	240	PROTEIN	30%
PROTEIN	20g	VITAMIN A	20%
CARBOHYDRATE	27g	VITAMIN C	6%
FAT	6g	THIAMINE	8%
CHOLESTEROL	70mg	RIBOFLAVIN	40%
SODIUM	510mg	NIACIN	10%
POTASSIUM	820mg	CALCIUM	50%
		IRON	45%

Chesapeake Oyster Bisque

Gumbos were developed as an economical and tasty way of using any combination of meat, fish, shellfish, vegetables, poultry or game. These one-pot meals, typical of the Cajuns and Creoles, represent southern Louisiana bayou cooking. The flavor and smooth texture of this chicken gumbo is achieved by the thickening properties of okra.

Southern Chicken Gumbo

    3 tablespoons margarine or
       butter
  ½ cup chopped onion
12-oz. pkg. frozen diced,
       precooked chicken or
       3 cups diced, cooked
       chicken
16-oz. can (2 cups) stewed
       tomatoes, cut up
  2½ cups chicken broth
10-oz. pkg. frozen cut okra or
       3 cups sliced fresh okra
  ¼ cup chopped parsley
    2 tablespoons lemon juice
    1 garlic clove, minced
  ⅛ teaspoon pepper
    3 drops hot pepper sauce
  ¼ cup uncooked regular rice

Melt margarine in large saucepan over medium heat. Cook onion and chicken until onion is tender and chicken is thawed. Add remaining ingredients except rice. Bring to a boil; stir in rice. Reduce heat; simmer uncovered for 20 minutes or until rice is tender.
4 (1¾-cup) servings.

▥ MICROWAVE DIRECTIONS: In 3-quart microwave-safe casserole, microwave margarine on HIGH for 30 seconds or until melted. Add onion and chicken; toss to coat. Cover tightly. Microwave on HIGH for 3 to 5 minutes or until onion is tender, stirring once halfway through cooking. Stir in **2 cups chicken broth** and remaining ingredients. Cover; microwave on HIGH for 12 to 18 minutes or until rice is thoroughly cooked, stirring twice during cooking.

NUTRITION INFORMATION PER SERVING

SERVING SIZE: 1-3/4 CUPS		PERCENT U.S. RDA PER SERVING	
CALORIES	340	PROTEIN	45%
PROTEIN	28g	VITAMIN A	30%
CARBOHYDRATE	24g	VITAMIN C	35%
FAT	15g	THIAMINE	15%
CHOLESTEROL	80mg	RIBOFLAVIN	15%
SODIUM	720mg	NIACIN	50%
POTASSIUM	710mg	CALCIUM	10%
		IRON	15%

The rich, distinctive flavor of black-eyed peas characterizes Hoppin' John, a dish often served in the South for New Year's Eve dinner. Here is a soup version of this Southern specialty.

Hoppin' John Soup

16-oz. pkg. (2½ cups) dry black-eyed peas
15 cups water
2 chicken-flavor bouillon cubes or 2 teaspoons instant chicken-flavor bouillon
1½ lb. ham shank
1 teaspoon oregano leaves
¼ teaspoon cayenne pepper
6 peppercorns or ¼ teaspoon pepper
1 garlic clove, minced
1 bay leaf
1 cup chopped onions
½ cup uncooked regular rice
2 green onions, sliced
Hot pepper sauce, if desired

Sort black-eyed peas. Rinse well; drain. In 5-quart Dutch oven, bring 8 cups of the water to a boil. Remove from heat; stir in black-eyed peas. Let stand uncovered 30 minutes to allow peas to expand. Bring to a boil. Boil 3 minutes. Remove from heat. Cover and let stand 1 hour; drain.

Add remaining 7 cups water, bouillon cubes, ham shank, oregano, cayenne, peppercorns, garlic and bay leaf. Bring to a boil.

Reduce heat; cover and simmer 1 to 1½ hours or until peas are tender. Remove ham shank, bay leaf and peppercorns. Stir in chopped onions and rice. Simmer covered an additional 25 to 30 minutes or until rice is tender. Remove meat from bone; cut into bite-sized pieces.

In small bowl, mash 1 cup cooked pea mixture with potato masher or fork. Stir mashed pea mixture and meat into peas in Dutch oven. Simmer until thoroughly heated. Sprinkle green onion slices on top of each serving. Pass hot pepper sauce to be added to individual servings as desired.
8 (1½-cup) servings.

NUTRITION INFORMATION PER SERVING

SERVING SIZE: 1-1/2 CUPS		PERCENT U.S. RDA PER SERVING	
CALORIES	280	PROTEIN	30%
PROTEIN	29g	VITAMIN A	4%
CARBOHYDRATE	46g	VITAMIN C	10%
FAT	2g	THIAMINE	45%
CHOLESTEROL	10mg	RIBOFLAVIN	10%
SODIUM	550mg	NIACIN	10%
POTASSIUM	760mg	CALCIUM	8%
		IRON	30%

This famous Southern stew has long been served in Kentucky on Derby Day and at other outdoor events where large crowds gather. When authentically prepared, the dish is simmered outdoors in huge iron caldrons over open fires. Our recipe, while smaller, does require a large stockpot. Don't worry about leftovers because Burgoo improves in flavor the following day.

Party Time Kentucky Burgoo

4 to 5	lb. mixed meat shanks (beef, pork, veal, and/or lamb)
3	lb. roasting or stewing chicken
4 to 5	quarts water
1	tablespoon salt
½	teaspoon pepper
4	cups diced, peeled potatoes
2	cups diced onions
2	cups diced, peeled turnips
2	cups chopped green cabbage
29-oz.	can tomato puree
2	tablespoons Worchestershire sauce
½	cup chopped fresh parsley or ¼ cup parsley flakes
16-oz.	pkg. Green Giant® Frozen Mixed Vegetables

Arrange shanks and chicken in 12-quart stockpot. Add enough water to just cover. Bring to a boil. Skim off any residue that rises to the surface. Reduce heat; cover and simmer until meat is tender, 2½ to 3 hours.

Remove meats and chicken. Cut meat and chicken from bones; discard skin and bones. Strain broth.* Cut meat and chicken into bite-sized pieces. Bring broth to a boil in stockpot. Add meat, chicken, salt, pepper, potatoes, onions, turnips, cabbage, tomato puree and Worchestershire sauce. Return to a boil. Reduce heat; cover and simmer until mixture thickens, 1 to 1½ hours. Stir in parsley and mixed vegetables. Cook 10 to 15 minutes or until mixed vegetables are crisp-tender. 22 (1½-cup) servings.

TIP: *To make ahead, at this point, recipe can be refrigerated for 24 hours. Store meat and chicken separately from broth. Remove fat from broth before completing recipe.

NUTRITION INFORMATION PER SERVING

SERVING SIZE: 1-1/2 CUPS		PERCENT U.S. RDA PER SERVING	
CALORIES	180	PROTEIN	35%
PROTEIN	22g	VITAMIN A	35%
CARBOHYDRATE	14g	VITAMIN C	35%
FAT	4g	THIAMINE	10%
CHOLESTEROL	50mg	RIBOFLAVIN	10%
SODIUM	330mg	NIACIN	25%
POTASSIUM	650mg	CALCIUM	4%
		IRON	15%

Pictured on previous page: Party Time Kentucky Burgoo

Originally a hunters' stew containing either squirrel or rabbit, this famous southern stew is now commonly made with chicken. Its origin is linked to Brunswick County, Virginia and it has traditionally been made in large quantities for political and social picnics. This family-sized version is as robust as the original recipe.

🍲 Brunswick Stew

½	cup chopped onion
1	medium green bell pepper, chopped
2	tablespoons margarine or butter
2	cups chicken broth
1	lb. cooked chicken, cut into 1-inch pieces
16-oz.	can (2 cups) whole tomatoes, undrained, cut up
15½-oz.	can butter beans, drained
7-oz.	can Green Giant® Niblets® Whole Kernel Golden Sweet Corn
⅛ to ¼	teaspoon crushed red pepper
½	cup sliced fresh or frozen okra
3	tablespoons flour
⅓	cup cold water
	Salt
	Pepper

In large saucepan, cook onion and green pepper in margarine until onion is tender. Stir in chicken broth, chicken, tomatoes, beans, corn and crushed red pepper; bring to a boil. Reduce heat; simmer 15 minutes. Add okra; simmer an additional 5 minutes or until okra is tender. In small jar with tight-fitting lid, add flour to cold water; shake well. Stir into stew mixture. Cook over medium heat until mixture boils and thickens, stirring frequently. Add salt and pepper to taste. 4 to 6 servings.

NUTRITION INFORMATION PER SERVING

SERVING SIZE: 1/6 OF RECIPE		PERCENT U.S. RDA PER SERVING	
CALORIES	300	PROTEIN	40%
PROTEIN	28g	VITAMIN A	15%
CARBOHYDRATE	23g	VITAMIN C	35%
FAT	10g	THIAMINE	10%
CHOLESTEROL	70mg	RIBOFLAVIN	10%
SODIUM	640mg	NIACIN	40%
POTASSIUM	650mg	CALCIUM	6%
		IRON	15%

Cook's Note

Garnishes for Soups and Stews

Garnishes for soups and stews can add texture, flavor and color in addition to decorative touches. Possibilities include: croutons, crackers, popcorn, sieved hard-cooked egg yolk, chopped or julienned vegetables, shredded or grated cheese, chopped nuts, lemon slices, fresh herbs, sour cream, crumbled cooked bacon or a sprinkle of a seasoning like nutmeg or paprika.

Oven Lovin' Breads

Oven Lovin'
Breads

The perfect partners for every soup or stew.

Bread, the staff of life, supports cassoulets, consommes, gumbos, burgoos, soups, stews and ragouts by providing complementary flavors, textures, and nutritional balance to a one-pot meal.

In this chapter, the breads have all been developed specifically with soups and stews in mind. You'll discover breads made in minutes using the microwave and convenience products, breads made with yeast and kneading, quick breads and spoon breads, breads made in time-saving batches and breads made hearty with whole grains.

Thanks in part to the popularity of Southwestern and health-conscious cookery, the "hot" grain for bread making is cornmeal. It has been fun for us to feature cornmeal in a variety of recipes. You'll find it in muffins, pan breads, dumplings and as a crisp topping for loaf breads. Available in yellow, white, or blue, the types are quite interchangeable, and the recipes in this book have been tested using all three. Blue cornmeal lends color interest to Tex-Mex dishes, but cornmeal crosses all cultures and goes equally well with *Brunswick Stew, Boston-Style Fish Chowder* and *Multi-Bean Soup.*

Recipes incorporating oats, rye, and whole wheat abound, too, in hearth-shaped loaves, pull-apart rolls and more.

Pictured on previous page: Bulgar Wheat Loaf

Serve this crusty round loaf with any of our soups or stews. The whole grain goodness comes from a combination of bulgur wheat and whole wheat flour.

Bulgur Wheat Loaf

- ¾ cup water
- ½ cup bulgur wheat
- 2¼ to 2½ cups Pillsbury's BEST® All Purpose or Unbleached Flour
- 2 tablespoons brown sugar
- 1 to 1½ teaspoons salt
- 1 pkg. active dry yeast
- 1 cup water heated to 120 to 130°F.
- ¼ cup oil
- 1 cup Pillsbury's BEST® Whole Wheat Flour
- 2 teaspoons water
- 1 egg white
- 1 teaspoon bulgur wheat

Grease cookie sheet. Bring ¾ cup water to a boil in small saucepan. Remove from heat; stir in ½ cup bulgur. Let stand 20 to 25 minutes or until water is absorbed. Lightly spoon flour into measuring cup; level off. In large bowl, combine 1 cup all purpose flour, brown sugar, salt, yeast, 1 cup hot water and oil; beat at low speed until moistened. Beat 3 minutes at medium speed. By hand, stir in bulgur mixture, whole wheat flour and additional 1 cup all purpose flour to form a stiff dough.

On floured surface, knead in ¼ to ½ cup all purpose flour until dough is elastic, about 5 minutes. Place in greased bowl; turn greased side up. Cover loosely with greased plastic wrap and cloth towel. Let rise in warm place (80 to 85°F.) until light and doubled in size, about 45 minutes.

Punch down dough several times to remove all air bubbles. Shape into round loaf. Place on greased cookie sheet. Cover; let rise in warm place until light and almost doubled in size, about 30 minutes.

Heat oven to 375°F. Uncover dough. With very sharp knife, cut a ½-inch deep slash across top of loaf. Cut another at a right angle, making a cross. In small bowl, beat 2 teaspoons water and egg white until blended. Brush over top of loaf; sprinkle with 1 teaspoon bulgur, if desired. Bake at 375°F. for 25 to 35 minutes or until golden brown. Remove from cookie sheet; cool on wire rack. 1 (17-slice) loaf.

HIGH ALTITUDE – Above 3500 Feet: Increase whole wheat flour to 1½ cups. Bake as directed above.

NUTRITION INFORMATION PER SERVING

SERVING SIZE:		PERCENT U.S. RDA	
1 SLICE		PER SERVING	
CALORIES	150	PROTEIN	6%
PROTEIN	4g	VITAMIN A	*
CARBOHYDRATE	24g	VITAMIN C	*
FAT	4g	THIAMINE	10%
CHOLESTEROL	0mg	RIBOFLAVIN	6%
SODIUM	130mg	NIACIN	8%
POTASSIUM	75mg	CALCIUM	*
		IRON	8%

*Contains less than 2% of the U.S. RDA of this nutrient.

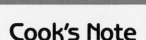

Cook's Note
About Bulgur

Bulgur is cracked partially-cooked wheat. Processing takes only a small part of the bran so bulgur is nutritionally identical to whole wheat. That means it contains dietary fiber, protein, iron, potassium and B vitamins. The high fiber content along with its chewy texture and nutty flavor make bulgur an intriguing bread addition. When making breads, it can be used as is or cooked. The most common way to cook bulgur is to use a 2:1 ratio of liquid, either stock or water, to the dry grain. Bring liquid to a boil in saucepan. Stir in bulgur; remove from heat. Cover and let stand 20 minutes or until bulgur absorbs the liquid. Look for bulgur in the bulk foods section or next to rice in the supermarket.

This moist, slightly sweet corn bread is so easy to make and microwave! Yellow, white and blue cornmeal are interchangeable; each produces a unique, top-quality corn bread.

Microwave Corn Bread

⅔ cup Pillsbury's BEST® All
    Purpose or Unbleached Flour
⅔ cup cornmeal
1 teaspoon baking powder
½ teaspoon baking soda
¼ teaspoon salt
3 tablespoons margarine or butter
½ cup buttermilk*
2 tablespoons honey
1 egg

TOPPING**
1 tablespoon cornmeal
2 teaspoons sugar

MICROWAVE DIRECTIONS:
Lightly spoon flour into measuring cup; level off. In medium bowl, combine flour, ⅔ cup cornmeal, baking powder, baking soda and salt; blend well. Set aside. In small microwave-safe bowl, microwave margarine on HIGH for 15 to 30 seconds or until melted. Stir in buttermilk, honey and egg until well blended. Add to flour mixture; stir just until dry ingredients are moistened. Pour into ungreased 8 or 9-inch round microwave-safe dish.

In small bowl, combine topping ingredients; blend well. Sprinkle over batter. Microwave on MEDIUM for 5 minutes, rotating dish once halfway through baking. Microwave on HIGH for 2 to 2½ minutes or until corn bread pulls away from sides of dish, rotating dish once halfway through baking. Let stand 5 minutes on flat surface. Cut into wedges. 6 to 8 servings.

TIPS: *To substitute for buttermilk, use 1½ teaspoons vinegar or lemon juice plus milk to make ½ cup.

    **When preparing recipe with blue cornmeal, omit topping.

HIGH ALTITUDE—Above 3500 Feet:
No change.

NUTRITION INFORMATION PER SERVING

SERVING SIZE: 1/8 OF RECIPE		PERCENT U.S. RDA PER SERVING	
CALORIES	150	PROTEIN	4%
PROTEIN	3g	VITAMIN A	4%
CARBOHYDRATE	22g	VITAMIN C	*
FAT	6g	THIAMINE	6%
CHOLESTEROL	35mg	RIBOFLAVIN	4%
SODIUM	250mg	NIACIN	4%
POTASSIUM	75mg	CALCIUM	4%
		IRON	4%

*Contains less than 2% of the U.S. RDA of this nutrient.

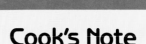

Cook's Note
About Cornmeal

By definition, cornmeal is ground dried corn kernels. Commercial cornmeal has the tough outer hull or bran of the corn kernel steamed away in the milling process. The germ is then removed leaving the endosperm to be ground by steel rollers into granules. The granules are separated by size: the large size called grits, the medium called cornmeal and the small called corn flour.

The color of cornmeal can be yellow, white or blue depending on the variety of corn. All three are generally interchangeable in recipes. However, when used in baking, blue cornmeal turns grayish-blue. Much of the blue cornmeal available is grown organically without chemicals or fertilizers in New Mexico. It is abundant in the Southwest or in other parts of the country in specialty stores or food co-ops.

Serve squares of this bright, colorful corn bread with Boston-Style Fish Chowder (see Index).

Corn-fetti Bread

1½ cups Pillsbury's BEST® All Purpose or Unbleached Flour
½ cup yellow cornmeal
2 tablespoons sugar
1 tablespoon baking powder
1 teaspoon salt
½ teaspoon dry mustard
½ cup milk
⅓ cup margarine or butter, melted
3 eggs, beaten
¼ cup finely chopped onion
¼ cup finely chopped green bell pepper
¼ cup finely chopped pimiento or red bell pepper
11-oz. can Green Giant® Niblets® Whole Kernel Golden Sweet Corn, drained

Heat oven to 425°F. Grease 9-inch square pan. Lightly spoon flour into measuring cup; level off. In medium bowl, combine flour, cornmeal, sugar, baking powder, salt and dry mustard; blend well. Stir in milk, margarine and eggs. Fold in onion, green pepper, pimiento and corn. Spoon batter into greased pan. Bake at 425°F. for 25 to 30 minutes or until toothpick inserted in center comes out clean. Serve warm. Store tightly covered in refrigerator. 9 servings.

HIGH ALTITUDE—Above 3500 Feet: Decrease baking powder to 2 teaspoons.

NUTRITION INFORMATION PER SERVING

SERVING SIZE: 1/9 OF RECIPE		PERCENT U.S. RDA PER SERVING	
CALORIES	230	PROTEIN	8%
PROTEIN	6g	VITAMIN A	10%
CARBOHYDRATE	31g	VITAMIN C	10%
FAT	10g	THIAMINE	10%
CHOLESTEROL	90mg	RIBOFLAVIN	10%
SODIUM	510mg	NIACIN	8%
POTASSIUM	160mg	CALCIUM	10%
		IRON	8%

Spoon bread, a popular Southern mealtime accompaniment, is a soft custard-like corn bread. Its moist souffle-like texture is at its best served immediately from the oven.

Spoon Bread with Corn

1½ cups water
1 cup white cornmeal
½ teaspoon salt
2 tablespoons margarine or butter
2 teaspoons baking powder
8-oz. carton plain nonfat yogurt
2 eggs, separated
7-oz. can Green Giant® Niblets® Whole Kernel Golden Sweet Corn, undrained

Heat oven to 375°F. Grease 1-quart souffle dish or 8-inch square baking pan. Bring water to a boil in medium saucepan. Slowly stir in cornmeal and salt. Cook 1 to 2 minutes or until mixture becomes very thick, stirring constantly. Remove from heat; stir in margarine. Gradually beat in baking powder, yogurt and 2 egg yolks. Stir in undrained corn. In small bowl, beat 2 egg whites until stiff. Fold into cornmeal mixture. Pour batter into greased dish. Sprinkle top with additional cornmeal, if desired. Bake at 375°F. for 40 to 50 minutes or until knife inserted near center comes out clean. 8 (½-cup) servings.

TIPS: Two teaspoons minced fresh sage or ½ teaspoon sage leaves can be added along with the corn.

Yellow or blue cornmeal can be substituted for white cornmeal.

HIGH ALTITUDE—Above 3500 Feet: No change.

NUTRITION INFORMATION PER SERVING

SERVING SIZE: 1/2 CUP		PERCENT U.S. RDA PER SERVING	
CALORIES	130	PROTEIN	6%
PROTEIN	5g	VITAMIN A	4%
CARBOHYDRATE	17g	VITAMIN C	*
FAT	5g	THIAMINE	4%
CHOLESTEROL	70mg	RIBOFLAVIN	8%
SODIUM	340mg	NIACIN	2%
POTASSIUM	150mg	CALCIUM	10%
		IRON	2%

*Contains less than 2% of the U.S. RDA of this nutrient.

The use of fast-acting yeast and the food processor will save you time in the preparation of these breadsticks. Fast-acting yeast reduces rising time and the food processor eliminates kneading. The breadsticks are easy to prepare while a pot of soup is simmering.

◗ Cornmeal Breadsticks

Cornmeal
1¾ to 2¼ cups Pillsbury's BEST® All Purpose or Unbleached Flour
1 cup cornmeal
¼ cup sugar
1 teaspoon salt
1 pkg. fast-acting dry yeast
1 cup water
¼ cup margarine or butter Melted margarine or butter

Grease 2 large cookie sheets; sprinkle with cornmeal. Lightly spoon flour into measuring cup; level off. In large bowl, combine 1 cup flour, 1 cup cornmeal, sugar, salt and yeast; blend well. In small saucepan, heat water and ¼ cup margarine until hot (120 to 130°F.). Add hot liquid to flour mixture. Blend at low speed until moistened; beat 2 minutes at medium speed. By hand, stir in ½ to 1 cup flour until dough pulls away from sides of bowl.

On floured surface, knead in ¼ cup flour until dough is smooth and elastic, about 2 minutes. Place dough in greased bowl; cover loosely with plastic wrap and cloth towel. Let rise in warm place (80 to 85°F.) until light and doubled in size, about 10 minutes.

Punch down dough several times to remove all air bubbles. Divide dough into 24 pieces; roll each into 10-inch rope. Place on greased cookie

sheets sprinkled with cornmeal. Cover; let rise in warm place until light and doubled in size, about 10 minutes.

Heat oven to 375°F. Uncover dough. Carefully brush sticks with melted margarine; sprinkle with cornmeal. Bake at 375°F. for 12 to 16 minutes or until bottoms are golden brown. Remove from pans immediately; cool on wire racks. 24 breadsticks.

🍞 FOOD PROCESSOR DIRECTIONS: In food processor bowl with metal blade, combine 1¼ cups flour, 1 cup cornmeal, sugar, salt, yeast and ¼ cup margarine. Cover; process 5 seconds. With machine running, pour **1 cup water heated to 120 to 130°F.** through feed tube; continue processing until blended, about 20 seconds. Add ½ to 1 cup flour; process 10 to 20 seconds longer or until stiff dough forms. With rubber scraper, carefully pull dough from blade and bowl; place in lightly greased bowl. Continue as directed above.

HIGH ALTITUDE — Above 3500 Feet: No change.

NUTRITION INFORMATION PER SERVING

SERVING SIZE: 1 BREADSTICK		PERCENT U.S. RDA PER SERVING	
CALORIES	110	PROTEIN	2%
PROTEIN	2g	VITAMIN A	2%
CARBOHYDRATE	17g	VITAMIN C	*
FAT	4g	THIAMINE	6%
CHOLESTEROL	0mg	RIBOFLAVIN	4%
SODIUM	130mg	NIACIN	4%
POTASSIUM	40mg	CALCIUM	*
		IRON	4%

*Contains less than 2% of the U.S. RDA of this nutrient.

Cornmeal Breadsticks

These savory cheese-filled breadsticks are from the 22nd Bake-Off® contest.

Crescent Cheese Breadsticks

3 tablespoons cornflake crumbs or crushed cornflakes
3 tablespoons grated Parmesan cheese
1 tablespoon parsley flakes
¼ teaspoon garlic salt
¼ teaspoon onion salt
¼ teaspoon chili powder
8-oz. can Pillsbury Refrigerated Quick Crescent Dinner Rolls
½ cup shredded Cheddar or American cheese
2 tablespoons butter or margarine, melted
½ teaspoon liquid smoke flavoring, if desired

Heat oven to 375°F. In shallow bowl, combine cornflake crumbs, Parmesan cheese, parsley flakes, garlic salt, onion salt and chili powder; set aside. Separate dough into 8 triangles; sprinkle with Cheddar cheese. Roll up, starting at shortest side of triangle, rolling **tightly** to opposite point. Roll to stretch each into a stick about 6 inches long. Combine butter and smoke flavoring. Roll sticks in butter mixture; coat with crumb mixture. Place seam side down on ungreased cookie sheet. Bake at 375°F. for 12 to 15 minutes or until golden brown. Serve warm. 8 breadsticks.

TIP: *To make ahead, prepare, cover and refrigerate up to 2 hours before baking. Bake as directed above.

NUTRITION INFORMATION PER SERVING

SERVING SIZE: 1 BREADSTICK		PERCENT U.S. RDA PER SERVING	
CALORIES	170	PROTEIN	6%
PROTEIN	5g	VITAMIN A	6%
CARBOHYDRATE	13g	VITAMIN C	*
FAT	11g	THIAMINE	6%
CHOLESTEROL	20mg	RIBOFLAVIN	6%
SODIUM	480mg	NIACIN	6%
POTASSIUM	85mg	CALCIUM	8%
		IRON	6%

*Contains less than 2% of the U.S. RDA of this nutrient.

There is no shaping needed for these yeast-leavened rolls. Instead, the batter is spooned into muffin cups. The resulting light, tender cornmeal rolls are the perfect accompaniment to Brunswick Stew (see Index).

Cornmeal Sesame Batter Rolls

1¾ to 2 cups Pillsbury's BEST® All Purpose or Unbleached Flour
½ cup white or yellow cornmeal
1 tablespoon sugar
1 teaspoon salt
1 pkg. active dry yeast
1 cup milk
¼ cup margarine or butter
1 egg
Sesame seed

Generously grease 12 muffin cups. Lightly spoon flour into measuring cup; level off. In large bowl, combine 1 cup flour, cornmeal, sugar, salt and yeast; blend well. In small saucepan, heat milk and margarine until hot (120 to 130°F.). Add hot liquid and egg to flour mixture. Blend at low speed until moistened; beat 2 minutes at medium speed. By hand, stir in ¾ to 1 cup flour to form a stiff batter. Cover batter; let rise in warm place (80 to 85°F.) until light and doubled in size, about 45 minutes.

Stir down batter; spoon into greased muffin cups. Sprinkle with sesame seed. Cover loosely with greased plastic wrap and cloth towel. Let rise in warm place until light and doubled in size, about 30 minutes.

Heat oven to 400°F. Uncover dough. Bake at 400°F. for 10 to 15 minutes or until golden brown. Remove from muffin cups immediately. 12 rolls.

HIGH ALTITUDE—Above 3500 Feet: No change.

NUTRITION INFORMATION PER SERVING
SERVING SIZE: PERCENT U.S. RDA
1 ROLL   PER SERVING
CALORIES   150   PROTEIN   6%
PROTEIN   4g   VITAMIN A   4%
CARBOHYDRATE   22g   VITAMIN C   *
FAT   5g   THIAMINE   10%
CHOLESTEROL   25mg   RIBOFLAVIN   10%
SODIUM   240mg NIACIN   6%
POTASSIUM   85mg   CALCIUM   2%
                        IRON   6%
*Contains less than 2% of the U.S. RDA of this nutrient.

These chewy rounds from versatile Pillsbury Refrigerated Soft Breadsticks are fabulous with Microwave White 'n Wild Rice Soup (see Index).

Sesame Rounds

11-oz. can Pillsbury Refrigerated
Soft Breadsticks
1 teaspoon water
1 teaspoon Dijon mustard
1 egg
4 teaspoons sesame seed

Heat oven to 425°F. Grease 2 cookie sheets. Separate but do not unroll breadsticks. Place coils 4 inches apart on greased cookie sheets. Press each coil to 5-inch circle; pinch to seal separations. Prick entire surface with fork. In small bowl, beat water, mustard and egg until well blended. Brush over circles of dough. Generously sprinkle with sesame seed. Bake at 425°F. for 7 to 10 minutes or until golden brown on edges. Serve warm. 8 rolls.

Sesame and Basil Rounds: Prepare rounds as directed above. Before sprinkling with sesame seed, place 1 medium fresh basil leaf on each round. Generously sprinkle surrounding area with sesame seed. Bake as directed above.

NUTRITION INFORMATION PER SERVING
SERVING SIZE: PERCENT U.S. RDA
1 ROLL   PER SERVING
CALORIES   120   PROTEIN   6%
PROTEIN   4g   VITAMIN A   *
CARBOHYDRATE   17g   VITAMIN C   *
FAT   4g   THIAMINE   100%
CHOLESTEROL   35mg   RIBOFLAVIN   6%
SODIUM   260mg NIACIN   6%
POTASSIUM   40mg   CALCIUM   *
                        IRON   6%
*Contains less than 2% of the U.S. RDA of this nutrient.

This recipe has become a Pillsbury favorite. To ensure success, eggs and milk must be at room temperature. All of our soups and stews go well with these golden brown, crusty popovers.

Perfect Popovers

3 eggs, room temperature
1¼ cups milk, room temperature
1¼ cups Pillsbury's BEST® All
Purpose or Unbleached
Flour
¼ teaspoon salt

Heat oven to 450°F. Generously grease 10 popover cups or ten 6-oz. custard cups.* In small bowl, beat eggs with rotary beater until lemon-colored and foamy. Add milk; blend well. Lightly spoon flour into measuring cup; level off. Add flour and salt; beat with rotary beater just until batter is smooth and foamy on top. Pour batter into greased cups, about ⅔ full. Bake at 450°F. for 15 minutes. (DO NOT OPEN OVEN.) Reduce heat to 350°F.; bake 25 to 35 minutes or until high, hollow and deep golden brown. Remove from oven; insert sharp knife into each popover to allow steam to escape. Remove from pan. Serve hot with butter. 10 popovers.

TIP: *Standard muffin pans can be used. Fill alternating greased cups with batter to prevent sides of popovers from touching.

HIGH ALTITUDE — Above 3500 Feet: Increase flour to 1¼ cups plus 2 tablespoons. Bake at 450°F. for 15 minutes and at 350°F. for 20 to 30 minutes.

NUTRITION INFORMATION PER SERVING
SERVING SIZE: PERCENT U.S. RDA
1 POPOVER   PER SERVING
CALORIES   90   PROTEIN   6%
PROTEIN   4g   VITAMIN A   2%
CARBOHYDRATE   14g   VITAMIN C   *
FAT   2g   THIAMINE   8%
CHOLESTEROL   80mg   RIBOFLAVIN   8%
SODIUM   90mg   NIACIN   4%
POTASSIUM   80mg   CALCIUM   4%
                        IRON   6%
*Contains less than 2% of the U.S. RDA of this nutrient.

This bountiful pull-apart bread is just as great the second day as the first. The moist, tender texture comes from hearty rolled oats. The tips below tell how this wonderful bread can fit into your lifestyle.

Herbed Oatmeal Pan Bread

2 cups water
1 cup rolled oats
3 tablespoons margarine
  or butter
3¾ to 4¾ cups Pillsbury's BEST®
  All Purpose or
  Unbleached Flour
¼ cup sugar
2 teaspoons salt
2 pkg. active dry yeast
1 egg

HERB TOPPING
1 tablespoon grated
  Parmesan cheese
½ teaspoon basil leaves
¼ teaspoon oregano
  leaves
¼ teaspoon garlic powder
6 tablespoons margarine
  or butter, melted

Grease 13x9-inch baking pan.* Bring water to a boil in medium saucepan; stir in rolled oats. Remove from heat; stir in 3 tablespoons margarine. Cool to 120 to 130°F.

Lightly spoon flour into measuring cup; level off. In large bowl, combine 1½ cups flour, sugar, salt and yeast; blend well. Add rolled oats mixture and egg. Blend at low speed until moistened; beat 3 minutes at medium speed. By hand, stir in 1¾ cups to 2½ cups flour to form stiff dough.

On floured surface, knead in ½ to ¾ cup flour until dough is smooth and elastic, about 5 minutes. Shape dough into ball; cover with large bowl. Let rest 15 minutes. Punch down dough several times to remove all air bubbles. Press into

greased pan. Using very sharp knife, cut diagonal lines 1½ inches apart, cutting completely through dough. Repeat in opposite direction creating diamond pattern. Cover loosely with greased plastic wrap and cloth towel.** Let rise in warm place (80 to 85°F.) until light and doubled in size, about 45 minutes.

Heat oven to 375°F. Uncover dough. Redefine cuts by poking tip of knife into cuts until knife hits bottom of pan; do not pull knife through dough. In small bowl, combine Parmesan cheese, basil leaves, oregano leaves and garlic powder; set aside. Spoon 4 tablespoons of the butter over cut dough. Bake at 375°F. for 15 minutes. Brush remaining 2 tablespoons of butter over partially-baked bread. Sprinkle with Parmesan cheese-herb mixture. Bake for an additional 10 to 15 minutes or until golden brown. Serve warm or cool. 16 servings.

TIPS: *Two 8 or 9-inch square pans or one 8-inch and one 9-inch square pan can be substituted for 13x9-inch pan. When using 2 square pans, one pan can be baked and the other pan refrigerated for baking the next day.

**To bake at a later time, at this point let stand at room temperature for 20 minutes. Remove cloth towel. Refrigerate 2 to 24 hours. Remove plastic wrap from dough; let stand at room temperature 30 minutes. Bake as directed above.

HIGH ALTITUDE—Above 3500 Feet: No change.

NUTRITION INFORMATION PER SERVING

SERVING SIZE: 1/16 OF RECIPE		PERCENT U.S. RDA PER SERVING	
CALORIES	240	PROTEIN	8%
PROTEIN	6g	VITAMIN A	6%
CARBOHYDRATE	35g	VITAMIN C	*
FAT	8g	THIAMINE	20%
CHOLESTEROL	15mg	RIBOFLAVIN	10%
SODIUM	350mg	NIACIN	10%
POTASSIUM	80mg	CALCIUM	2%
		IRON	10%

*Contains less than 2% of the U.S. RDA of this nutrient.

Herbed Oatmeal Pan Bread

Cut this flatbread into sticks or squares to serve with soups, salads or meats.

Tomato and Herb Flatbread

2 tablespoons cornmeal, if desired
1 pkg. Pillsbury Hot Roll Mix
⅓ cup Hungry Jack® Mashed Potato Flakes
1⅓ cups water heated to 120 to 130°F.
2 tablespoons margarine or butter, softened
1 egg
¼ cup Italian tomato paste or tomato paste
1 tablespoon olive oil
1 teaspoon Italian seasoning
Coarse ground black pepper, if desired

Grease 15x10x1-inch baking pan. Sprinkle with cornmeal. In large bowl, combine flour mixture with yeast from foil packet and potato flakes; blend well. Stir in **hot** water, margarine and egg until dough pulls cleanly away from sides of bowl. With greased fingers, pat dough into bottom of greased pan sprinkled with cornmeal. In small bowl, whisk together tomato paste, olive oil and seasoning. Spread evenly over top of dough. Cover with greased plastic wrap. Let rise in warm place (80 to 85°F.) 30 minutes.

Heat oven to 375°F. Uncover dough. Sprinkle black pepper over tomato paste mixture. Bake at 375°F. for 15 to 20 minutes or until golden brown. 24 servings.

HIGH ALTITUDE—Above 3500 Feet: No change.

NUTRITION INFORMATION PER SERVING

SERVING SIZE: 1/24 OF RECIPE		PERCENT U.S. RDA PER SERVING	
CALORIES	90	PROTEIN	4%
PROTEIN	3g	VITAMIN A	2%
CARBOHYDRATE	16g	VITAMIN C	2%
FAT	2g	THIAMINE	8%
CHOLESTEROL	10mg	RIBOFLAVIN	6%
SODIUM	170mg	NIACIN	6%
POTASSIUM	70mg	CALCIUM	*
		IRON	4%

*Contains less than 2% of the U.S. RDA of this nutrient.

Add spark to your meal with this flavorful flatbread. For those who don't enjoy the hot "bite" of crushed red pepper, adjust the level accordingly.

Rosemary and Red Chili Focaccia

1 pkg. Pillsbury Hot Roll Mix
2 tablespoons finely chopped fresh rosemary or 1 tablespoon rosemary, crushed
1½ to 2 teaspoons crushed red pepper
1 cup water heated to 120 to 130°F.
2 tablespoons olive or vegetable oil
1 egg
2 teaspoons water
1 egg

Grease large cookie sheet or 12-inch pizza pan. In large bowl, combine flour mixture with yeast from foil packet, rosemary and red pepper; blend well. Stir in 1 cup **hot** water, olive oil and 1 egg until dough pulls away from sides of bowl. Turn dough out onto lightly floured surface. With greased or floured hands, shape dough into a ball. Knead dough 5 minutes until smooth. Cover with large bowl; let rest 5 minutes.

Place dough on greased cookie sheet. Roll or press into 12-inch circle. Cover loosely with greased plastic wrap and cloth towel. Let rise in warm place (80 to 85°F.) 30 minutes.

Heat oven to 375°F. Uncover dough. In small bowl, combine 2 teaspoons water and 1 egg; beat well. Brush thin layer over top of dough. With handle of wooden spoon or fingers, poke holes over entire surface of dough at 2-inch intervals. Bake at 375°F. for 15 to 25 minutes or until

golden brown. Remove from cookie sheet; cool on wire rack.
1 (20-slice) loaf.

HIGH ALTITUDE—Above 3500 Feet: No change.

NUTRITION INFORMATION PER SERVING

SERVING SIZE: 1 SLICE		PERCENT U.S. RDA PER SERVING	
CALORIES	100	PROTEIN	4%
PROTEIN	3g	VITAMIN A	2%
CARBOHYDRATE	17g	VITAMIN C	*
FAT	2g	THIAMINE	10%
CHOLESTEROL	25mg	RIBOFLAVIN	8%
SODIUM	160mg	NIACIN	6%
POTASSIUM	45mg	CALCIUM	*
		IRON	4%

*Contains less than 2% of the U.S. RDA of this nutrient.

Full of nutritious ingredients, these tasty muffins have a light moist texture and tempting appeal.

Oats 'n Wheat Blueberry Muffins

- 1 cup quick-cooking rolled oats
- 1¼ cups buttermilk*
- ½ cup honey
- ¼ cup oil
- 1 egg, slightly beaten
- 1½ cups Pillsbury's BEST® Whole Wheat Flour
- 1 teaspoon baking soda
- ½ teaspoon salt
- 1 cup fresh blueberries or frozen blueberries without liquid, thawed

In large bowl, combine rolled oats and buttermilk; mix well. Let stand 5 minutes. Heat oven to 375°F. Grease 12 muffin cups or line with paper baking cups. Stir honey, oil and egg into rolled oats mixture; mix well. Lightly spoon flour into measuring cup; level off. In small bowl, combine whole wheat flour, baking soda and salt; blend well. Add to rolled oats mixture; stir just until dry ingredients are moistened. Fold in blueberries. Fill greased muffin cups about ¾ full. Bake at 375°F. for 20 to 25 minutes or until toothpick inserted in center comes out clean. 12 muffins.

📖 MICROWAVE DIRECTIONS: Prepare muffin batter as directed above. Using 6-cup microwave-safe muffin pan, line each cup with 2 paper baking cups to absorb moisture during baking. Fill cups ½ full. Microwave on HIGH for 2½ to 3¼ minutes or until toothpick inserted in center comes out clean, rotating pan ½ turn halfway through baking. Remove muffins from pan and immediately remove outer baking cups. Cool 1 minute on wire rack before serving. Repeat with remaining batter making 6 additional muffins. With remaining batter, make 3 muffins; microwave 3 muffins on HIGH for 1½ to 2 minutes. 15 muffins.

TIP: *To substitute for buttermilk, use 1 tablespoon plus 1 teaspoon vinegar or lemon juice plus milk to make 1¼ cups.

HIGH ALTITUDE—Above 3500 Feet: Increase whole wheat flour to 1¾ cups. Bake as directed above.

NUTRITION INFORMATION PER SERVING

SERVING SIZE: 1 MUFFIN		PERCENT U.S. RDA PER SERVING	
CALORIES	190	PROTEIN	6%
PROTEIN	5g	VITAMIN A	*
CARBOHYDRATE	30g	VITAMIN C	2%
FAT	6g	THIAMINE	10%
CHOLESTEROL	25mg	RIBOFLAVIN	4%
SODIUM	220mg	NIACIN	4%
POTASSIUM	140mg	CALCIUM	4%
		IRON	4%

*Contains less than 2% of the U.S. RDA of this nutrient.

Fresh parsley adds flavor and visual appeal to these French bread slices. They're topped with Monterey jack cheese and are a wonderful accompaniment to soups and stews.

Country French Bread Slices

¼ cup margarine or butter, softened
1 tablespoon chopped fresh parsley or 2 teaspoons parsley flakes
8 (1-inch) slices French bread
4 oz. (4 slices) Monterey jack or brick cheese
Parsley

Heat oven to 400°F. In small bowl, combine margarine and parsley. Spread on one side of each bread slice. Place, buttered side down, on ungreased 15x10x1-inch baking pan or cookie sheet. Toast in 400°F. oven for 5 minutes; turn bread slices buttered side up. Cut each slice of cheese into 4 squares. Place 2 squares of cheese on top of each bread slice. Bake for an additional 2 to 3 minutes or until cheese is melted. Garnish with fresh chopped parsley, if desired. 8 slices.

NUTRITION INFORMATION PER SERVING

SERVING SIZE: 1 SLICE		PERCENT U.S. RDA PER SERVING	
CALORIES	210	PROTEIN	10%
PROTEIN	7g	VITAMIN A	8%
CARBOHYDRATE	20g	VITAMIN C	*
FAT	11g	THIAMINE	8%
CHOLESTEROL	15mg	RIBOFLAVIN	8%
SODIUM	350mg	NIACIN	6%
POTASSIUM	50mg	CALCIUM	10%
		IRON	6%

*Contains less than 2% of the U.S. RDA of this nutrient.

These rich savory scones get their tender texture from whipping cream rather than butter or shortening. We think this easy recipe is one you will want to make often.

Basil-Parmesan Scones

1¼ to 1½ cups Pillsbury's BEST® Self-Rising Flour*
3 tablespoons oat bran
2 tablespoons grated Parmesan cheese
1 teaspoon basil leaves
1 cup whipping cream
1 teaspoon oat bran

Heat oven to 425°F. Grease cookie sheet. Lightly spoon flour into measuring cup; level off. In large bowl, combine 1¼ cups flour, 3 tablespoons oat bran, Parmesan cheese and basil; blend well. Reserve 1 teaspoon whipping cream. Add remaining cream to flour mixture, stirring just until soft dough forms. If dough is too wet, stir in flour, one tablespoon at a time.

On floured surface, knead gently to form smooth ball. Place on greased cookie sheet. Pat or roll to 6-inch circle. Cut into 8 wedges; do not separate. Brush with reserved 1 teaspoon whipping cream; sprinkle with 1 teaspoon oat bran. Bake at 425°F. for 15 to 18 minutes or until lightly browned. 8 scones.

TIP: *Pillsbury's BEST® All Purpose or Unbleached Flour can be substituted for self-rising flour. Add 2 teaspoons baking powder and ½ teaspoon salt.

HIGH ALTITUDE—Above 3500 Feet: No change.

NUTRITION INFORMATION PER SERVING

SERVING SIZE: 1 SCONE		PERCENT U.S. RDA PER SERVING	
CALORIES	200	PROTEIN	6%
PROTEIN	4g	VITAMIN A	8%
CARBOHYDRATE	20g	VITAMIN C	*
FAT	12g	THIAMINE	10%
CHOLESTEROL	40mg	RIBOFLAVIN	8%
SODIUM	40mg	NIACIN	6%
POTASSIUM	60mg	CALCIUM	4%
		IRON	6%

*Contains less than 2% of the U.S. RDA of this nutrient.

Basil-Parmesan Scones

News of oat bran as a tool to help lower cholesterol has encouraged many cooks to add it to their recipes. Here at Pillsbury we have found a subtle way to incorporate this great fiber into a crusty loaf of one of America's favorite breads.

⦿ Oat Bran French Bread

1	tablespoon cornmeal
2¼ to 2¾	cups Pillsbury's BEST® All Purpose or Unbleached Flour
⅓	cup oat bran hot cereal, uncooked
1	pkg. active dry yeast
1	teaspoon salt
1	cup water heated to 120 to 130°F.
1	tablespoon honey
½	teaspoon cornstarch
¼	cup water

Grease cookie sheet; sprinkle with cornmeal.* Lightly spoon flour into measuring cup; level off. In large bowl, combine 1 cup flour, oat bran cereal, yeast and salt; blend well. Add 1 cup hot water and honey to flour mixture. Blend at low speed until moistened; beat 3 minutes at medium speed. By hand, stir in 1 to 1¼ cups flour to form a stiff dough.

On floured surface, knead in ¼ to ½ cup flour until dough is smooth and elastic, about 5 minutes. Shape dough into ball; place in greased bowl and turn to grease top. Cover with plastic wrap and cloth towel. Let rise in warm place (80 to 85°F.) 30 minutes.

Punch down dough several times to remove all air bubbles. Shape dough by rolling back and forth on counter into a 15-inch long loaf. Place on greased cookie sheet sprinkled with cornmeal. Cover; let rise in warm place until almost doubled, about 15 minutes.

Heat oven to 400°F. In small saucepan, combine cornstarch and ¼ cup water; mix well. Bring to a boil; cook until mixture is thickened and clear. Remove from heat; cool, stirring occasionally. Uncover dough. With very sharp knife, cut four ½-inch deep diagonal slashes on top of loaf. Brush loaf with a thin layer of cornstarch mixture. Bake at 400°F. for 10 minutes. Brush with cornstarch mixture again. Bake an additional 15 to 20 minutes or until golden brown and loaf sounds hollow when lightly tapped. Immediately remove from cookie sheet; cool on wire rack.
1 (15-slice) loaf.

🍽 FOOD PROCESSOR DIRECTIONS: Grease cookie sheet; sprinkle with cornmeal.* Sprinkle yeast over ¼ **cup water heated to 105 to 115°F.** Stir in honey. Let stand until foamy, about 5 minutes. Lightly spoon flour into measuring cup; level off. In food processor bowl with metal blade, combine 2¼ cups flour, oat bran cereal and salt; process to blend. Stir ⅔ **cup water heated to 105 to 115°F.** into yeast mixture. With motor running, pour yeast mixture through feed tube in a steady stream as fast as flour absorbs it. When dough forms a ball, stop machine. Dough should feel slightly sticky. If dough is too wet, add flour by tablespoons with motor running; if too dry, add water by teaspoons until well blended. Knead by processing continuously for 45 seconds. Continue as directed above.

TIP: *French bread stick pans can be substituted for cookie sheet. Grease pans; sprinkle with cornmeal. To shape bread, divide dough in half. Gently elongate each half by rolling back and forth to 1 inch shorter than length of pan. Place in greased pans. Continue as directed above.

HIGH ALTITUDE—Above 3500 Feet: No change.

NUTRITION INFORMATION PER SERVING
SERVING SIZE: PERCENT U.S. RDA
1 SLICE   PER SERVING
CALORIES   90   PROTEIN   4%
PROTEIN   3g   VITAMIN A   *
CARBOHYDRATE   19g   VITAMIN C   *
FAT   0g   THIAMINE   10%
CHOLESTEROL   0mg   RIBOFLAVIN   6%
SODIUM   140mg   NIACIN   6%
POTASSIUM   40mg   CALCIUM   *
                       IRON   6%
*Contains less than 2% of the U.S. RDA of this nutrient.

The best thing about making your own bread is that you can serve it warm from the oven. Serve this with a steaming bowl of soup to chase away winter chills.

Hearty Oats 'n Wheat Loaves

2 to 2½ cups Pillsbury's BEST® All Purpose or Unbleached Flour
1 cup rolled oats
2 teaspoons salt
3 pkg. active dry yeast
1¾ cups water
½ cup corn syrup
½ cup margarine or butter
2 eggs (1 separated)
2 cups Pillsbury's BEST® Whole Wheat Flour
1 cup Pillsbury's BEST® Medium Rye Flour
1 tablespoon water
4 teaspoons sesame seed

Lightly spoon flour into measuring cup; level off. In large bowl, combine 1½ cups all purpose flour, rolled oats, salt and yeast; blend well. In medium saucepan, heat 1¾ cups water, corn syrup and margarine until hot (120 to 130°F.). Add hot liquid, one egg and one egg yolk (reserve egg white) to flour mixture. Blend at low speed until moistened; beat 3 minutes at medium speed. By hand, stir in whole wheat flour and rye flour to form a soft dough. On floured surface, knead in ½ to 1 cup all purpose flour until dough is smooth and elastic, about 10 minutes. Place dough in greased bowl; cover loosely with plastic wrap and cloth towel. Let rise in warm place (80 to 85°F.) until light and doubled in size, about 1 hour.

Generously grease two 8x4 or 9x5-inch loaf pans. Punch down dough several times to remove all air bubbles. Divide dough into 2 parts; shape into loaves. Place in greased pans. Cover; let rise in warm place until light and doubled in size, about 1 hour.

Heat oven to 375°F. Uncover dough. In small bowl, combine reserved egg white and 1 tablespoon water; brush over loaves. Sprinkle with sesame seed. Bake 30 to 40 minutes or until golden brown and loaves sound hollow when lightly tapped. Remove from pans immediately. Cool on wire racks. 2 (12-slice) loaves.

HIGH ALTITUDE—Above 3500 Feet: Decrease yeast to 2 packages. Bake as directed above.

NUTRITION INFORMATION PER SERVING
SERVING SIZE: PERCENT U.S. RDA
1 SLICE   PER SERVING
CALORIES   180   PROTEIN   6%
PROTEIN   5g   VITAMIN A   2%
CARBOHYDRATE   28g   VITAMIN C   *
FAT   5g   THIAMINE   10%
CHOLESTEROL   25mg   RIBOFLAVIN   8%
SODIUM   230mg   NIACIN   8%
POTASSIUM   95mg   CALCIUM   *
                       IRON   8%
*Contains less than 2% of the U.S. RDA of this nutrient.

Take a shortcut using Pillsbury Hot Roll Mix to achieve two chewy loaves of this old-time German bread. It is delicious with Shrimp Wild Rice Soup (see Index).

Pronto Pumpernickel

1 pkg. Pillsbury Hot Roll Mix
¾ cup Pillsbury's BEST® Medium
    Rye Flour
1½ teaspoons caraway seed
½ teaspoon instant coffee
    granules or crystals
1¼ cups water heated to 120 to
    130°F.
¼ cup dark molasses
2 tablespoons margarine or
    butter, softened
2 eggs (1 separated)
½ teaspoon caraway seed

Grease cookie sheet. Lightly spoon flour into measuring cup; level off. In large bowl, combine flour mixture with yeast from foil packet, rye flour and 1½ teaspoons caraway seed; blend well. In measuring cup, dissolve coffee granules in **hot** water. Stir hot coffee, molasses, margarine, 1 egg and 1 egg yolk (reserve egg white) into flour mixture until dough pulls cleanly away from sides of bowl. Turn dough out onto floured surface. With greased or floured hands, shape dough into a ball. Knead dough 5 minutes until smooth. Cover dough with large bowl; let rest 5 minutes.

On lightly floured surface, divide dough in half. Flatten each half into 12x7-inch rectangle. Starting at 7-inch side, roll up firmly. Pinch ends to seal; place, seam side down, 4 to 6 inches apart on greased cookie sheet. Cover loosely with greased plastic wrap and cloth towel. Let rise in warm place (80 to 85°F.) until light and doubled in size, about 45 minutes.

Heat oven to 350°F. Uncover dough. With very sharp knife, cut three ½-inch deep, diagonal slashes on top of each loaf. Brush with reserved egg white. Sprinkle each loaf with ¼ teaspoon caraway seed. Bake at 350°F. for 25 to 35 minutes or until deep golden brown.
2 (16-slice) loaves.

HIGH ALTITUDE—Above 3500 Feet: Increase rye flour to 1 cup. Bake as directed above.

NUTRITION INFORMATION PER SERVING

SERVING SIZE: 1 SLICE		PERCENT U.S. RDA PER SERVING	
CALORIES	80	PROTEIN	2%
PROTEIN	2g	VITAMIN A	*
CARBOHYDRATE	14g	VITAMIN C	*
FAT	1g	THIAMINE	6%
CHOLESTEROL	15mg	RIBOFLAVIN	4%
SODIUM	110mg	NIACIN	4%
POTASSIUM	55mg	CALCIUM	*
		IRON	4%

*Contains less than 2% of the U.S. RDA of this nutrient.

Pronto Pumpernickel

Enjoy these buttery rolls with Salmon 'n Vegetable Chowder (see Index).

Butter Crisp Garlic Rolls

1 pkg. Pillsbury Hot Roll Mix
1 teaspoon garlic salt
1 teaspoon instant minced onion
⅛ teaspoon savory or thyme
   leaves
1 cup water heated to 120 to
   130°F.
2 tablespoons margarine or
   butter, softened
1 egg
¼ teaspoon garlic salt
2 tablespoons margarine or
   butter, melted

Generously grease 13x9-inch pan. In large bowl, combine flour mixture with yeast from foil packet, 1 teaspoon garlic salt, onion and savory; mix well. Stir in **hot** water, 2 tablespoons softened margarine and egg until dough pulls away from sides of bowl.

Turn dough out onto lightly floured surface. With greased or floured hands, shape dough into a ball. Knead dough for 5 minutes until smooth. Cover dough with large bowl; let rest 5 minutes.

Press dough evenly into greased pan. In small bowl, combine ¼ teaspoon garlic salt with 2 tablespoons melted margarine.

Dipping sharp knife into margarine mixture before each cut, cut dough lengthwise down center and then crosswise at 1-inch intervals, making 2 rows of 13 strips. Brush rolls with remaining margarine mixture. Cover loosely with plastic wrap and cloth towel. Let rise in warm place (80 to 85°F.) 30 minutes.

Heat oven to 375°F. Uncover dough. Bake at 375°F. for 20 to 25 minutes or until deep golden brown. Immediately remove from pan. Serve warm. 26 rolls.

HIGH ALTITUDE—Above 3500 Feet: No change.

NUTRITION INFORMATION PER SERVING

SERVING SIZE: 1 ROLL		PERCENT U.S. RDA PER SERVING	
CALORIES	80	PROTEIN	2%
PROTEIN	2g	VITAMIN A	*
CARBOHYDRATE	13g	VITAMIN C	*
FAT	2g	THIAMINE	8%
CHOLESTEROL	10mg	RIBOFLAVIN	6%
SODIUM	230mg	NIACIN	4%
POTASSIUM	30mg	CALCIUM	
		IRON	2%

*Contains less than 2% of the U.S. RDA of this nutrient.

A batter bread is an easy way to prepare a yeast-leavened bread. The use of the food processor makes this recipe even easier. Enjoy this bread's mild nacho flavor with Smoked Ham and Lentil Soup (see Index).

◊ Food Processor Nacho Batter Bread

- 1 pkg. active dry yeast
- ¼ cup water heated to 105 to 115°F.
- 2 cups Pillsbury's BEST® All Purpose or Unbleached Flour
- 1 cup Pillsbury's BEST® Whole Wheat Flour
- 3 tablespoons cornmeal
- ½ teaspoon salt
- ½ teaspoon garlic powder
- ¼ teaspoon cumin
- 1 tablespoon margarine or butter, softened
- 10½-oz. can condensed nacho cheese soup
- 1 egg
- ½ teaspoon poppy seed

🍳 FOOD PROCESSOR DIRECTIONS: Generously grease 1½-quart casserole or souffle dish.

In 1-cup measure, dissolve yeast in warm water. Lightly spoon flour into measuring cup; level off. In food processor bowl with metal blade, combine all purpose flour, whole wheat flour, cornmeal, salt, garlic powder, cumin and margarine. Cover; process to combine. Add soup, egg and yeast mixture. Cover; process 20 to 30 seconds or until dough forms a ball. If dough is too wet, add flour by tablespoons with motor running; if too dry, add water by teaspoons until well blended. With plastic scraper, carefully pull dough from blade and bowl; place in greased casserole. Sprinkle top with poppy seed; gently press in dough. Cover loosely with plastic wrap and cloth towel. Let rise in warm place (80 to 85°F.) until light, 1 to 1¼ hours.

Heat oven to 375°F. Uncover dough. Bake at 375°F. for 30 to 40 minutes or until golden brown. Remove from casserole immediately; cool on wire rack. 1 (18-slice) loaf.

HIGH ALTITUDE—Above 3500 Feet: No change.

NUTRITION INFORMATION PER SERVING

SERVING SIZE: 1 SLICE		PERCENT U.S. RDA PER SERVING	
CALORIES	100	PROTEIN	4%
PROTEIN	4g	VITAMIN A	4%
CARBOHYDRATE	17g	VITAMIN C	*
FAT	2g	THIAMINE	8%
CHOLESTEROL	15mg	RIBOFLAVIN	4%
SODIUM	170mg	NIACIN	6%
POTASSIUM	55mg	CALCIUM	2%
		IRON	6%

*Contains less than 2% of the U.S. RDA of this nutrient.

This version of the popular Mexican bread, Peineta, is easy to make with our hot roll mix. It pairs perfectly with Multi-Bean Soup (see Index).

Zesty Cheese Comb Bread

1 pkg. Pillsbury Hot Roll Mix
¼ cup cornmeal
¼ teaspoon cayenne pepper
4 oz. (1 cup) shredded sharp Cheddar cheese
1 cup water heated to 120 to 130°F.
2 tablespoons oil
2 tablespoons honey
1 egg

Grease large cookie sheet. In large bowl, combine flour mixture with yeast from foil packet, cornmeal, cayenne pepper and cheese; blend well. Stir in **hot** water, oil, honey and egg until dough pulls away from sides of bowl. With greased or floured hands, shape dough into a ball. Knead in any remaining dry ingredients until dough is smooth. Place dough on lightly floured surface. Cover dough with large bowl; let rest 5 minutes.

Cut dough in half. Roll each half into 9-inch circle. Transfer circles onto large greased cookie sheet. Using scissors, make ¾-inch cuts ½ inch apart around edges of dough circles. For each loaf, fold dough circle over (not quite in half) so that both cut edges are visible. Cover loosely with greased plastic wrap and cloth towel. Let rise in warm place (80 to 85°F.) 30 minutes.

Heat oven to 350°F. Uncover dough. Bake at 350°F. for 18 to 28 minutes or until golden brown and loaves sound hollow when lightly tapped. Brush lightly with oil, if desired. Remove from cookie sheet; cool on wire rack. 2 (7-slice) loaves.

HIGH ALTITUDE—Above 3500 Feet: No change.

Pictured top to bottom: Multi-Bean Soup p. 16, Zesty Cheese Comb Bread

NUTRITION INFORMATION PER SERVING

SERVING SIZE: 1 SLICE		PERCENT U.S. RDA PER SERVING	
CALORIES	180	PROTEIN	10%
PROTEIN	6g	VITAMIN A	2%
CARBOHYDRATE	28g	VITAMIN C	*
FAT	5g	THIAMINE	15%
CHOLESTEROL	30mg	RIBOFLAVIN	10%
SODIUM	280mg	NIACIN	10%
POTASSIUM	65mg	CALCIUM	6%
		IRON	6%

*Contains less than 2% of the U.S. RDA of this nutrient.

Jumbo Dilled Cornmeal Muffins

½ cup Pillsbury's BEST® All Purpose or Unbleached Flour
½ cup Pillsbury's BEST® Whole Wheat Flour
1 cup cornmeal
1 tablespoon baking powder
½ teaspoon salt
1 cup milk
¼ cup oil
3 tablespoons honey
2 tablespoons finely chopped fresh dill weed or
  1 tablespoon dill weed
1 egg

Heat oven to 400°F. Grease six 6-oz. custard cups or 12 muffin cups. Lightly spoon flour into measuring cup; level off. In large bowl, combine all purpose flour, whole wheat flour, cornmeal, baking powder and salt; blend well. In small bowl, combine milk, oil, honey, dill weed and egg; mix well. Add to dry ingredients; stir just until moistened. Spoon batter evenly into greased custard cups.* Bake at 400°F. for 15 to 18 minutes or until toothpick inserted in center comes out clean. Cool 1 minute; remove from custard cups. Serve warm. 6 muffins.

TIP: *For easier handling, place custard cups on rimmed cookie sheet.

HIGH ALTITUDE—Above 3500 Feet: No change.

NUTRITION INFORMATION PER SERVING

SERVING SIZE: 1 MUFFIN		PERCENT U.S. RDA PER SERVING	
CALORIES	300	PROTEIN	10%
PROTEIN	7g	VITAMIN A	4%
CARBOHYDRATE	42g	VITAMIN C	*
FAT	12g	THIAMINE	10%
CHOLESTEROL	50mg	RIBOFLAVIN	10%
SODIUM	360mg	NIACIN	6%
POTASSIUM	200mg	CALCIUM	15%
		IRON	8%

*Contains less than 2% of the U.S. RDA of this nutrient.

Nutrition Information

Pillsbury's NUTRI-CODED system can help you in your daily food planning. Below are guidelines:

SERVING SIZE: This has been determined as a typical serving for each recipe.

CALORIES: The amount of calories a person needs is determined by age, size and activity level. The recommended daily allowances generally are: 1800-2400 for women and children 4 to 10 years of age and 2400-2800 for men.

PROTEIN: The amount of protein needed daily is determined by age and size; the general U.S. RDA is 65 grams for adults and children of at least 4 years of age.

CARBOHYDRATE, FAT, CHOLESTEROL, SODIUM, AND POTASSIUM: Recommended Daily Allowances (RDA) for these nutrients have not been determined; however, the carbohydrate should be adequate so the body does not burn protein for energy.

Smoked Ham and Lentil Soup p. 19

The American Heart Association recommendation for those who wish to restrict dietary cholesterol is for a daily intake that is less than 100 milligrams per 1000 calories and not exceeding a total of 300 milligrams.

PERCENT U.S. RDA PER SERVING: For a nutritionally balanced diet, choose recipes which will provide 100% of the U.S. Recommended Daily Allowance for each nutrient.

Pillsbury Guidelines for Calculating the Nutrition Information:

• When the ingredient listing gives one or more options, the first ingredient listed is the one analyzed.

• When a range is given for an ingredient, the larger amount is analyzed.

• When ingredients are listed as "if desired," these ingredients are included in the nutrition information.

• Serving suggestions listed in the ingredients are calculated in the nutrition information.

• When each bread recipe is analyzed, a serving of yeast-leavened bread is a 1-oz. slice and a quick bread serving is 1/16 of the loaf. Recipes that vary are indicated.

Symbol Meanings:

The following symbols are used in relation to the nutrition data:

*	Less than 2% of the nutrient
<1	Less than one gram (or milligram) of the nutrient

Any questions regarding nutrition information in this book should be addressed to:

The Pillsbury Company
Pillsbury Center — Suite 2866
Minneapolis, Minnesota 55402

The primary source for values used in this program is the revised Agriculture Handbook No. 8. The values are only as correct and complete as the information supplied.

NOTE FOR PEOPLE WITH SPECIAL DIETARY NEEDS: CONSULT YOUR PHYSICIAN REGARDING RELIANCE ON THE NUTRITION INFORMATION IN THIS BOOK.
Every effort has been made to ensure the accuracy of this information. However, The Pillsbury Company does not guarantee its suitability for specific medically imposed diets.

Index

Index

Index

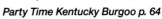

Party Time Kentucky Burgoo p. 64

OUR NEW BAKING COOKBOOK IS CAUSING QUITE A STIR,

This is it. *The Complete Book of Baking.* The only book on baking you'll ever need. It's filled with hundreds of Pillsbury tested recipes. But it's so much more than just great recipes.

Pillsbury's new cookbook is so complete, we could have called it the encyclopedia of baking. Inside you'll find valuable "how-to" tips on everything from freezing various baked goods to mailing cookies!

This special 8 x 10-inch hardcover edition contains 512 pages of recipes, tips and nutritional information, plus over 150 color photos and instructive illustrations.

It all adds up to the most comprehensive book on baking available.

And it can be yours for only $16.95!* That's a 30% savings from the suggested retail price. At this great price, you'll want one for yourself and one for gift-giving.

Don't hesitate – order today while supply lasts.

ONLY $16⁹⁵

ORDER FORM

	Qty.	Total
The Complete Book of Baking (A $25.00 Value) Only $16.95 x _____	=	$ _____

** *Shipping and handling fees included for U.S. (Canada and other countries, please add $3.00 per book)*

☐ Check or money order enclosed *(U.S. funds only)* ☐ Charge my Visa, MasterCard or Discover

Card # ☐☐☐☐ ☐☐☐☐ ☐☐☐☐ ☐☐☐☐   Expires___ /_

Signature _____

(required for credit card orders only)

Name_____

Address _____

City_____ State _____ Zip_____

Send order to:
Pillsbury Baking Book Offer, Dept. 8090
1001 N. 4th Street, LeSueur, MN 56058
Please allow 6-8 weeks for delivery. Offer good while supply lasts.

PILLSBURY PUBLICATIONS